IN PURSUIT OF LEGACY

THREE KEYS TO ENDURING LEADERSHIP

Michael J. Claudio

WESTBOW
PRESS®
A DIVISION OF THOMAS NELSON
& ZONDERVAN

WestBow Press books may be ordered through booksellers or by contacting:

WestBow Press
A Division of Thomas Nelson & Zondervan
1663 Liberty Drive
Bloomington, IN 47403
www.westbowpress.com
1 (866) 928-1240

ISBN: 978-1-9736-8869-3 (sc)
ISBN: 978-1-9736-8870-9 (hc)
ISBN: 978-1-9736-8868-6 (e)

Library of Congress Control Number: 2020905610

Print information available on the last page.

WestBow Press rev. date: 5/12/2020

Never underestimate the importance of a 'great first impression'. Great leaders like Mike Claudio define that structure, which attracts engagement and buy in. *In Pursuit of Legacy* provides fundamental tools to drive growth and development for any leader.

Rich Lee, Principal RLee Consulting (RLee.Consulting)
Former Vice President for multiple automotive Tier 1 companies

Because he is a former baseball player, I am comfortable saying, "Mike hit a home run with this one." This book provides great, practical tips to help managers and leaders at any level grow. The book is well organized and can be used as a reference manual to assist readers in the future. I am glad to say <u>In Pursuit of Legacy</u> helped me think about how I lead in my companies.

Alfonzo Alexander
CEO, Alexander Success Group

"The shelves are full of leadership books by highly reputable authors. So, why would you pick this one up? **Mike Claudio** is an unknown amongst the great authors----but his impact on those he has served and supported in the trenches is profound. His greatest gift to the reader is his battle scars. On life's journey, from captain of the Middle School basketball team to the Executive Suite, Mike discovered that *managing ourselves well, managing others with purpose and intent, and inspiriting others through service and humility lays a firm foundation for leading a life of legacy. In Pursuit of Legacy* breathes life into Mike's heartfelt commitment to business, his family, and personal spiritual growth.

Dewey Greene
Managing Chair, C12 Group Nashville TN

May our pursuit be
all for Him who called
us to serve.

CONTENTS

INTRODUCTION

Leadership. There are a million ways to pursue perspectives on leadership, and most of them contain valuable information about steps to take or characteristics to demonstrate to be a good leader. Legacy, on the other hand, is a little more distant. It is more elusive to get a grasp on what makes someone a legacy leader.

John Maxwell calls this the Pinnacle leader (*5 Levels of Leadership*), the most difficult level of leadership to accomplish due to the characteristics and time and effort it takes. It requires developing leaders as well as followers, developing leaders to develop other leaders.

Jim Collins calls this the Level 5 leader (*Good to Great*). Collins says that the Level 5 leader creates enduring greatness through a perceived paradox of professional will and personal humility. They provide sufficient guidance and accountability while getting out of the way when credit is given.

There are other well-crafted definitions for this ultimate leader accomplishment, but you get the idea from these definitions. Few of us will ever reach such a pinnacle to be recognized in leadership books or *Harvard Business Review* articles, but we all have the opportunity to achieve a level of legacy leadership. Our circle of influence may be smaller, but the lasting impact of our efforts can be just as long and just as powerful as any recognized in the leadership journals of time.

This book contains the keys to behavioral characteristics that are foundational to enduring leadership. In my career, I have experienced and witnessed that those who adhered to these behavioral characteristics became effective leaders and flourished, while those who didn't struggled to get lasting results. The successful ones developed leaders around them and enjoyed the fruits of their investment of time and effort.

It is fortunate that as we grow and develop in our experiences and careers, our understanding and expectations transform as well. Wisdom is a combination of knowledge and experience. As a young man, I thought being a leader was a destination, a place to arrive. It is a good thing we are told to enjoy the journey, because what I have learned is that leadership is just that—a journey, and a potentially rocky journey at that.

My leadership journey started in athletics when I was elected captain of the middle school basketball team. Though not earth-shattering in itself, it did provide the first glimpse of what effective leadership requires. Some more life lessons came as I was fired from my first job out of college for not demonstrating some of the characteristics defined in this book. Having been on this journey for some time now, working for international brands and starting and running my own business for more than fifteen years, I have found that the challenges for a leader seem to reset almost every day.

About midway through my journey as a business owner, we expanded into a new revenue stream that was focused on technical staffing and recruiting. Our original business was in technical contracting but was more project based, and the staffing model was not something with which we had experience. We had some success but found ourselves stuck with stagnant growth and low profitability after nearly four years of operation. In the assessment of our situation, we identified a number of factors impacting our performance, and through that analysis, the concept for this book was initiated. Trying to capture the essence of what it takes to be an enduring leader in simple and actionable characteristics became the outline in that initial presentation. Today, that business unit is an effective team producing exceptional results.

In my research, I came across a word that perfectly describes the characteristics of what we wanted our team to understand about their roles in our success: Alaka'i. Alaka'i is the Hawaiian value of leadership, and it is a quality both in managing and leading (from *The 19 Values of Aloha* by Rosa Say). Being a successful leader requires management skills *and* leadership skills. *The Pursuit of Legacy* puts these leadership skills and characteristics into three buckets: managing yourself, managing others, and leading others.

We will explore all of these critical characteristics in more detail through the following pages and hopefully finish our exercise with a clearer picture about where each of us is on the pendulum of leadership.

Finally, this book is a reminder of the things that we know we should do; we may have lost sight of how we are doing in keeping up with these critical leadership characteristics. As Pat Lencioni said during one of his keynote presentations, "I am the chief reminder of what we should be doing." I am echoing his sentiments in that these principles are not new but simple reminders of the benefits of sticking to the basics. When we stick to the basics with intent to grow those around us, we make strides toward a pursuit of legacy.

LEADERSHIP KEY #1:
MANAGING YOURSELF

Discipline yourself, and others won't need to.
—John Wooden

MANAGING YOURSELF

We are always on stage. The honor and privilege to lead is earned through how we manage ourselves and hold ourselves accountable to a standard of performance that drives others to follow our example. While we are not perfect, our body of work has to speak loudly enough that those who look to us for guidance can look without wondering if our leadership is genuine and true.

The transition from just managing your own performance to that of managing a team of people includes an important aspect of historical perspective that is critical to achieve positive results at the next level. Surprisingly, some people forget how they used to perform once given the role of leader. This phenomenon of forgetting the performance efforts that helped an individual to be selected for a leadership role can be linked to immaturity, pride, ego, or simply misunderstanding the steps to succeed as a first-time leader. Quite simply, one must elevate personal discipline, not relax, during this transition to leadership.

How one manages their own attitudes and behaviors is critical to their ability to be successful in the other functions of leadership: managing and leading others. We will identify some key characteristics that provide a path to success by focusing on our behavior as it relates to impactful leadership.

How we manage ourselves is a stepping-stone to receiving the respect and admiration from those who are under our care. We earn that respect by acknowledging and demonstrating the characteristics that are critical to excellent performance and not just demanding it from our team. Earning the right to challenge others to achieve their own excellence and potential through self-management can only come from living it ourselves.

Model the way. Our actions that reinforce our words provide the motivation and confirmation for those who look to us for direction and encouragement to grow themselves.

ATTITUDE

There are a few things in our life where we have total control over how things turn out. One of the things we can demonstrate almost total control over is our attitude. Regardless of the circumstances surrounding us at the moment, we still get to choose how we let external inputs influence the energy and outlook we project. Granted, we all have an emotional quotient. Continuing stressful circumstances can certainly impede our approach to decision-making. Identifying when things are dragging your attitude down is an important skill to master.

Much of how we behave depends on the factors we are giving credence to in our psyche. The challenge we all face is how to appropriately filter the changing inputs into our psyche that can influence this critical performance driver called attitude. Each day, we get to choose our attitude.

Representative Sam Johnson of Texas was a fighter pilot for the US Air Force during the Vietnam conflict and was shot down and captured in 1966. He spent seven years as a POW, including nearly four years in solitary confinement, and he reflects on the importance of attitude to get through the worst of situations with the following statement: "We must choose to keep a positive attitude. And sometimes we have to make that choice many times throughout the day."

The power of a positive attitude in Representative Johnson and his colleagues who suffered the same fate helped them to endure the unthinkable and return home.

Most of us will never come close to having to muster up a positive attitude under similar circumstances, but in our own world of problems and unexpected situations, we must choose to maintain the proper attitude. There is good news and bad news with this scenario.

The good news is we get to choose how we display our attitude.

The bad news is we get to choose how we display our attitude.

We can't blame anyone or anything for our attitude choice!

The other main feature to understand about our attitude is the fact that whatever attitude we project is contagious, whether positive or negative. Our team can read what attitude we are exuding, and most people will respond in kind to what we do. If we respond negatively to results or circumstances, that response will get repeated and, unfortunately, probably magnified. If, however, we respond with a positive assessment of the news, we provide a buffer to the potential negative response from our team. While we don't control how people react to news and information, we do have a level of influence on the magnitude of those responses.

Maintaining a positive attitude is a learning process. Our internal stability helps us to create the capacity for a positive attitude. While some people have a calmer demeanor than others, attitude is an emotion that can be bolstered or hindered through teachers, mentors, and colleagues. Identifying those in your circle who demonstrate the skill you desire as it relates to attitude and learning from them will help strengthen your understanding of this emotion. If you don't have someone in your circle of influence who possesses this skill, look to expand your circle.

There is a great line in the movie *Remember the Titans* when the two leading players on the integrating football team are exchanging blame for how poorly the team is coming together. "Attitude reflects leadership, Captain" was the phrase used by the newcomer to the established team captain. What followed was a transformation of a group of young men who witnessed their leaders shift their attitude toward the situation and join forces to overcome their obstacles.

While the story is fictional, it is based on a true story of Coach Herman Boone during the integration of school systems in

Virginia during the 1970s. Coach Boone created an environment where his team could respond to his positive attitude toward their circumstances. If you haven't seen the movie, I won't ruin it for you here, but it is a great look at the power of attitude.

Renowned author John C. Maxwell puts it this way: "People may hear your words, but they feel your attitude."

Assess how you react to circumstances, both positive and negative, and determine how to become the conduit of positive impact through managing your attitude.

MEASURING ATTITUDE

On a scale from 1 to 5, with 5 being the goal, assess how you are doing as it relates to managing your attitude.

Level 1

> Seems like a rainy day every day. Seldom seems like anything is going well. Usually a grim look and demeanor.

Level 2

> Wears the circumstances of the moment on their sleeve. It is obvious if things are going well or going poorly.

Level 3

> Keeps an even keel on display regardless of good or bad situations.

Level 4

> Usually keeps a positive focus on events and circumstances. Encourages others to look at the bright side of situations.

Level 5

> Most of the time, this person has a bright outlook on how things will turn out and encourages others to keep their chin up. Others always feel better after being around them.

EFFORT

It is said that the difference between good and excellent is simply a decision to perform the task at hand with the time and care to make the result excellent. It is seldom more knowledge or training or skill, just purely more effort. Give me a group of people dedicated to giving 100 percent effort, and we will outperform a group of more talented and skilled people who are dedicated to just being good enough almost every time.

Note: A discussion of what excellence looks like could be a particularly long rabbit chase, but I want to point out that understanding the basis of excellence in a world of numbers and comparison can cause confusion about what excellence should be measured against. Dewey Greene, a successful health care professional and mentor, said the best method of measuring success was against opportunity. We may beat the budget by 20 percent, but if we could have beaten the budget by 30 percent with the respective opportunities that exist, should we still grade ourselves as performing with excellence? A good discussion to have as it relates to metrics!

Additionally, effort is like attitude; we have all of the control in this category of performance. No boss, coworker, subordinate, or customer can determine what effort I will give each day. I am responsible for my own effort!

As a basketball coach for thirteen years (volunteer only, talk about a hard profession!), one of the key elements I focused on with my players was effort. Hustle plays, a loose ball on the floor, fifty-fifty opportunities to regain possession, taking a charge and getting back into the play after a mistake—these were what I focused on when assessing potential players and what I drilled into my teams. We would often pass over a more talented player skill wise, who lacked in the effort column, to select a player with good skill but who gave great effort. Those players who have the effort commitment tend to be much more coachable and predictable in their performance. The same goes for our employees.

There are few things more frustrating than having to deal with a talented person who is not putting forth the effort expected. It is true for managers as well, and we have to recognize that the case is the same for our subordinates. There is little that is more frustrating for an employee than to see their boss underperforming due to lack of effort.

As mentioned earlier, as leaders, we are always on stage, and effort is one of those areas where people are always measuring our performance. Do we take plays off? What I mean is, is there a noticeable difference in our intensity and effort on some tasks and engagements compared to other situations? If there is, we are opening ourselves to having our team members question our consistency in effort. It is hard to expect or demand high effort if we are not willing to give it ourselves.

Effort is one of those things that we need to establish as a personal core value and decide well in advance of performing what we will hold ourselves accountable to achieve. If we wait until the moment of decision about whether to stick to the task or let it go as is, we open ourselves to situational commitment. If it is convenient and we have the energy to make it excellent, then we will push through, but if we don't feel it and performing is an inconvenience, we may let mediocre results pass. A decision to do it with excellence ahead of time is needed to get us through those moments. Our brain will find a way to give our body the strength to complete the task if we have decided that whatever it takes to deliver excellence is what we have committed.

Now let's look back to the stage. If we are committed to deliver excellence no matter what it takes, our team witnesses the energy and effort we deliver, and they take note. Here is where the value of your effort is multiplied. When you are willing to live up to that standard of excellence in your effort, those who work with you and for you will respond in kind. I know that, as a leader of people, there is little that is more rewarding than seeing a group of people who look to you for direction and leadership come together and accomplish great results through intense effort and commitment. Effort is one of the performance multipliers in business. The more ingrained effort becomes in a team, the more it is reciprocated by other team members.

Effort is one of the performance multipliers in business.

Not only is effort a key business element, but it is also a key element in a balanced life. While our job and business consume a major portion of our existence, planning and exerting focused effort toward our family, our marriage, our community, and our church or civic organization provides a long-lasting return in fulfilment, joy, and happiness. Remembering to be diligent and purposeful with our effort in these areas provides mental and emotional balance for us to be great at work.

MEASURING EFFORT

Level 1

Does the least amount of work, regardless of what is needed or desired to accomplish.

Level 2

Does only the amount of work needed to get the minimum acceptable outcome to expectations.

Level 3

Shows glimpses of high energy, but usually only on topics that are of interest or easy to complete.

Level 4

Can be counted on to work hard on most projects and encourages others to perform to high standards.

Level 5

Brings a high level of can-do spirit to almost every task or project.

TIME MANAGEMENT

With contributions by Aaron Adcock

Stroll through any bookstore, and you're bound to stumble across the self-help and advice section covering every topic you could possibly imagine about improving your business. Among these books, you'll undoubtedly find an entire shelf dedicated to time management. There is no shortage of advice on this topic, and like most people, I've flipped through several books desperately searching for the most effective approach to time management. I won't lie; I'm looking for the easy button, the secret, an ah-ha moment.

In all my research, albeit informal and with no resemblance to scientific theory, I've found the answer to effective time management. My study involves countless hours of thumbing pages in the aisles of a bookstore, and I've even made a few purchases. This is where you'll want to grab a pen and paper or highlighter, as I'm about to share the answer. Prioritizing your work and planning your day is the secret to effective time management.

Huge letdown, right? I know. That's how I felt. This isn't a secret, and most people would arrive at this conclusion on their own anyway. Everything I read, everywhere I looked, advice on time management always pointed to prioritizing your work and effectively planning your day. For most, including me, this is difficult at times. But it's a skill we already have; we just choose to not always use it. Think about your weekend. I assume most of you reading this don't lie in bed till noon and then get up only to be at the mercy of the day. You prioritize, and you plan. Kids have a basketball game at 9:00 a.m., and here is the list of groceries I will get right after I finish getting the oil changed in the car this afternoon.

Everyone is busy, and in most situations, time management has the potential to become an issue when your day has even the slightest disruption, caused by anything you didn't expect or plan for. Often, the unexpected disruptions present in the form of emails, phone calls, people, or issues that fall outside of the normal course of your business day.

The list is long, but the one disruption that is often overlooked is us. Individually, you are accountable for how you manage your day and handle these disruptions. How? By being disciplined in prioritizing your work, planning your day, and allotting time to accomplish what's most important. If you need a schedule, create one. If you need reminders, set them up. You are responsible.

I guess, in some respect, there is an easy button for time management. The problem lies with us, and so does the solution. It doesn't rely on others or the ability to go learn some complex skill that needs to be mastered. It only requires a pen and paper and a little bit of thought about what is most important in your day, whether it is business reports or groceries or basketball games. Prioritize that list, plan accordingly, and be disciplined in following through.

Be disciplined in prioritizing your work, planning your day, and allotting time to accomplish what's most important.

Some of you are saying, "Man, if I could do that, things would be just fine." If you find yourself struggling to become the valiant time manager, then take some other important steps to help this topic not be a hindrance for your success. The simplest, though not necessarily the easiest, is to surround yourself with people who make your weaknesses irrelevant.

When it comes to time management, identify those people who have the gift of discipline. My office manager, Laura, was just that for me over the past few years I ran my business. She was very disciplined, and her skills and focus on timing and follow-up were very beneficial for me, because it is an area where I do not have a natural skill set.

Another useful tool I have seen utilized is the Eisenhower Urgent versus Important matrix for decision-making. Urgency can be a leech on your time if the filter of importance is not applied to decision-making. See the chart below to help you assess how you are making decisions about where to give your time and make sure the important things are driving those decisions.

	Urgent	Not Urgent
Important	1 DO Pay Lease Payroll Safety/Quality/Compliance	2 PLAN Strategic Plan New Product New Benefit
Not Important	3 DELEGATE Meeting Host Data Entry Social Media	4 ELIMINATE Excess Meetings Excess Phone Time Procrastination

What is important is seldom urgent, and
what is urgent is seldom important.
—Dwight D. Eisenhower, thirty-fourth
president of the United States

MEASURING TIME MANAGEMENT

Level 1

Seems to always be in a bind for time and doesn't complete tasks on schedule.

Level 2

Usually doesn't have a plan regarding utilization of time and resources.

Level 3

Is effective the most part, but seems scattered at times regarding projects and timelines.

Level 4

Has things in order most of the time and completes tasks and projects by the due date.

Level 5

Utilizes excellent planning skills and usually completes tasks and projects ahead of schedule.

COMMITMENT

Some of the foundational components of our company (EHD Technologies) were the core values we established. We utilized the initials of the company, EHD, to create them: *excellence, honesty,* and *dedication*. (We initially started out with "extremely handsome dudes," but we didn't feel that totally captured the essence of what we were trying to accomplish, so we abandoned that idea.)

Commitment is a synonym for dedication. We added some clarity to our core values a few years later and came up with this definition for dedication: *to be all-in—attitude in action*. We spoke earlier about the importance of maintaining a positive attitude, and as you can see in the definition, attitude carries over into commitment through our actions.

You can learn a lot about people and their motivations when the going gets tough and the easy becomes difficult and mundane. Business owners learn early on in the process of starting and growing a business that commitment is required to be successful. There are very few businesses that succeed without significant drive and commitment from the business owners and leaders to see the company through the dark periods. Commitment to accomplish the objectives set out when the company was founded drives the owner to do whatever it takes, to be all-in, in order to succeed.

Commitment is initially a reflection of a person's internal compass. Some people will do whatever it takes to get the job done, just because that is how they were raised, and they have modeled their individual performance to emulate this upbringing. (We would all like to have a staff full of these types of people, but there aren't that many kids available for hire who were raised on a farm anymore.)

Second, commitment is a measure of an individual's buy-in to a purpose that is greater than their individual goal.

For managers and leaders, commitment is a *testament to whether they have a grasp on the purpose* for themselves and their team. Purpose is what gives the aspiring leader the ammunition and encouragement to complete the current tasks with energy and passion. There will always be rapids and rough waters in business and in leadership. Helping the team embrace the purpose of their actions by demonstrating commitment to the purpose provides strength and support during difficult times.

On a recent white-water rafting trip down the Ocoee River (great class 4/5 river, by the way) with my leadership team, I encountered a learning moment on the journey. Our guide instructed us through the rocks and rising water with humorous calls to paddle or push our way down the course, but she also instilled a certain amount of caution so that we respected the power of the water flowing so angrily below us. She continued to provide calmness and motivation, saying that she would guide us to the bottom of the river where we could enjoy the cool water and bask in the energy that completing the rapids brings. We would make it down the river.

On one section of the river, she recommended that we not fall out of the raft but wait until a later section of the river to get our fill of the water. Unfortunately, I wasn't paying close enough attention to her wise instruction and found myself bounding over the side of the raft, holding on only to my paddle and life vest. I had paid enough attention to the initial instruction and tried to keep my feet elevated so as not to get caught in any rocks, but I also bobbed like a fishing lure for the next hundred yards or so down the river. Wide-eyed and a little water heavy, I was pulled back into the raft by my colleagues with heavy breath and an elevated heart rate. "Wow!" I said. "She was right when she said to not fall out of the raft in that section." As we slowly drifted through the calm waters of the river leveling out to the lake level, I remembered what she promised at the top of the rapids:

we would make it down the river. And she was right. The feeling of accomplishment (and relief!) was evident in the whole party. Her commitment to get us down the river was realized.

Commitment is a testament to whether we have a grasp on the purpose of our role or not.

I have heard commitment referred to as *focused purpose*. Each of us must determine how we will direct our behavior and our attitude to accomplish the desired purpose. Good leaders provide the example of how to establish the focused purpose for those around them.

Renowned basketball coach John Wooden put it this way: "Discipline yourself, and others won't need to." Not much to add to that statement.

MEASURING COMMITMENT

Level 1

Tends to show a dis-interested, take-it or leave-it attitude to the assigned tasks.

Level 2

Is inconsistent in completing to a standard. Sometimes does great work, other times substandard work is performed.

Level 3

Will get things done to the minimally acceptable level, but will not typically stay engaged after that point is achieved.

Level 4

Usually will continue on task until all critical items are completed to a level above standard.

Level 5

Puts forth a "whatever it takes" attitude toward the task or project at hand; won't stop until excellence is achieved.

POLICIES AND PROCEDURES

I am not sure why companies have to institute policies and procedures. Well, I guess I know why: because people are people. Me too. Adhering to company policy as a manager of people is a critical component to being effective. Taking the "Do as I say, not as I do" approach with your direct reports has the potential to be a rocky, if not catastrophic, path.

As a freshly graduated engineer from Tennessee Tech University, I found myself at the employ of Duracell Battery in Cleveland, Tennessee. My first position was in the quality lab performing material characteristic testing for the plastic resin we received for the battery assembly, all on the first shift. Melt flow analysis, ash content, elasticity, impact resistance, and burn rate characteristics were some of the normal tests we would conduct on the different resins coming to the facility. Just what I had studied in college. Perfect.

Then the call came to my supervisor, announcing my next assignment: production shift supervisor for the third shift.

Duracell had been a long-standing place of employment in the community, and many of the employees there had served for a number of years. I was now in charge of about thirty people in the powder room mixing area for the 11:00 p.m. to 7:00 a.m. shift. The first issue was I had never worked an off shift before, and something just didn't seem right about sleeping during the day and leaving for work just before the late news finished. That would certainly require some behavioral adjustments. The second issue was I was twenty-four years old, fresh out of college with an engineering degree, and I was now responsible for a shift of employees whose average length of service with Duracell was nearly twenty years! There were team members on my shift who had worked for Duracell longer than I had been alive, and now I was directing the performance of the shift. Quite an eye-opener and exactly *not* what I had studied for in college.

There were some really great people on that shift who supported my transition into the supervisor role, and without their support, it would have been an unbearable burden. I had a chance to learn firsthand the struggles of attendance, resource allocation, and employee morale.

My assignment on the third shift lasted a few months, and then I found myself on the second shift in the same department. This is where the struggles truly began. The second shift was from 3:00 p.m. to 11:00 p.m. Monday to Friday. These were the same hours I had most looked forward to for the previous ten years: high school finished around 3:00 p.m., and in college, *The Andy Griffith Show* was often on during that time as well. Something not to miss! Now I was packing my lunch, which was actually dinner, and heading off to work. Oh, and I was recently married at that time as well. My wife worked normal hours, and I was now at work by the time she got home. It was not a great way to start off as a new couple, not seeing each other except on the weekends. Oh, and one more thing. My high school was about a half a mile away from the plant, and on Friday nights, I could hear the cheers of the crowd while on my lunch break. Just a few years earlier, I was playing football on that very field. Truly a combination of circumstances that led to some poor decisions on my part.

Okay, now back to policies. I don't remember exactly which policies I chose not to hold dearly to my heart during this period, but let's just say I might have bent the rules a little. I would have my wife—my new wife, I remind you—join me for lunch at the plant some evenings. My shift leader would cover for me, but we only had a brief period for lunch, twenty minutes, so I would stretch that out on these occasions. While I don't recall any employee-related issues with this behavior, my boss had some things to say about my actions. After an initial reprimand and continued stretching of the rules, I was terminated. What? Me, the get along with anyone, excel at almost everything, able to handle adversity with a smile, done? Yep. Out. What an eye-opener.

Setting the example in following the guidelines and policies is a fundamental step in effective managing.

As I reflected on the experience, what I noticed was my lapse in performing my duties as a manager in having my team follow the policies and procedures according to the rules. I didn't hold them accountable to the rules because I wasn't holding myself accountable to the rules. In my case, the issue became my personal problem, but in many cases, it becomes a daily struggle to police your team according to the policies.

Setting the example when it comes to following the guidelines and policies is a fundamental step in effective managing. If we introduce doubt into the management equation regarding what policies we will enforce and what policies we won't enforce, we invite our team to make their own choices about which ones they will adhere to as well. Save yourself some struggles and make this a priority in your daily management.

MEASURING COMMITMENT TO POLICIES AND PROCEDURES

Level 1

> Does not hold policies and procedures as requirements to follow.

Level 2

> Adheres to the policies that are agreeable with personal commitment levels, but does not sustain consistent adherence to other policies.

Level 3

> Demonstrates inconsistency in adherence to all policies and procedures.

Level 4

> On occasion has wavered from the policy requirements but mostly keeps in adherence.

Level 5

> Adheres to the policies and procedures and the intent for which they were written.

ENERGY

Energy can neither be created nor destroyed. I learned that from my enjoyable classes in physics during my study of engineering. That being said, energy can be transferred from one body to another, and it is a reality of human nature to pull energy from someone else.

In sports, we see it all the time. It's called momentum. One team member expels an extra amount of effort and energy to accomplish a task, and the other members of the team respond in kind with their own elevated effort. The net result is a period of time when the unit has exercised an above-normal level of output, and typically this leads to elevated performance. It seldom lasts for very long, but the effects of one person's influence on the group are obvious.

You can witness this in the business world as well. Name the person you know who, whenever they interject into a meeting or group of people, the energy level of the whole group goes up. It seems as if the group magically receives an influx of cosmic energy, and they respond to the positive impact of the person's input. I have witnessed this impact on numerous occasions. A group is working at a mundane task when someone comes in and brings energy to what they are doing, and suddenly the whole group picks up their pace and excitement. The group completes the task and celebrates the ensuing result with exuberance and comradery.

I experienced this firsthand as a young athlete. Coach Donnie Yates was that guy for me. He was my football coach in high school and taught Sunday school for many years. He was a man of humility and passion and energy. I mean energy. Donnie was the Energizer

Bunny before the Energizer Bunny became a thing. He was masterful at speaking life into young men and teaching them to embrace the coaching they were receiving and to adapt their behaviors. Young men would grab hold of this energy, and you would see amazing transformations from the beginning of summer practice to the first Friday-night game. Donnie was a catalyst of energy.

On the flip side, energy can be taken from people as well. Name that person everyone tries to avoid, finding another avenue down the hallway when they see that person coming. Is that you? I hope not. Nothing is more detrimental to team performance than a manager who zaps energy from a room.

So, what is important for a leader to bring to the group? Consistency. Your team needs to have a level of expectation about where you will typically be when it comes to energy. When you have large swings of effort from day to day or week to week, people don't know what to expect from you. This leads to doubt and often criticism. This doesn't mean you have to be something you are not. Some people are high-strung, high-energy people, and it seems they have a naturally made "press here for caffeine" button that exists somewhere on their person.

We have a sales guy who opens each week with a burst of inspiration to the sales team with his never-ending energy blasts.

> **If you're gonna be a bear, be a grizzly! Arrgghh!**
> **—Ronnie Pruett**

Find the correct level of energy that fits your personality and that you are comfortable bringing on a consistent basis. There will be days when you fall below that level, and certainly there will be days when you rise above that level and provide the bolt of energy that gives your team momentum.

MEASURING ENERGY

Level 1

> Seems to always need one more cup of coffee to get going, regardless of what time of day it is.

Level 2

> Maintains a consistent, low-level involvement and energy output.

Level 3

> Delivers an adequate amount of energy for the situation. Sometimes low key and sometimes high energy.

Level 4

> Keeps a high level of engagement and builds commitment from others to get things done.

Level 5

> Substitutes for the Energizer Bunny as needed! Always seems to be in high gear and gives a boost to others' energy levels.

MISSION / VISION / CORE VALUE BUY-IN

Understanding the *why* for ourselves is probably the most fundamental aspect of effective leadership. We see many business owners who have not been deliberate in creating clear direction for their team when it comes to why they exist and what purpose they have in doing what they do. For large companies, it becomes even harder to create that strong corporate culture that people across the organization embrace and live out on a consistent basis.

In his book *Start with Why*, Simon Sinek points out the critical need for connecting people to something greater than just making money. When people are connected to the purpose of the organization, the emotional motivations of an individual magnify the efforts, focus, and commitment he or she brings to their job. This concept is one of the most powerful tools in an organization but is so difficult to implement and sustain. Why? Because it is hard to create and hard to measure. It is hard to know how people are connecting with your purpose.

Here's the rub. You can't give something to someone that you haven't got yourself. If you haven't embraced the mission / vision / core values (M/V/CV) of your company or division, your people know it. You can't fake it in this area. When it comes to the difficult decisions, if you are not committed to the M/V/CV, then what you are committed to will come to the surface. As we stated earlier in the book, you are always on stage, and in no other category will you be more scrutinized by your team than in this area. Either the M/V/CV are top priorities, or they are just words on the wall.

You can't give something to someone that you haven't got yourself.

Excellence, honesty, and dedication were the core values we established in our company shortly after we started the organization. For each of these core values, we had to establish expectations around what it meant and how it would be lived out in the marketplace and in the office.

Excellence has some variance in measurement and completion, but the basic definition we came up with was to be extraordinary. John Wooden said, "Greatness comes from doing the ordinary things extraordinarily well."

Dedication also has some room for interpretation. We simply categorized this core value in this way: whatever it takes to complete the task at hand. *Whatever it takes* allows for the variation in expectations from our customers, but this definition provided clearly what we expected from our team members.

Honesty is very cut and dry. There are no variations in the expectations in this category. You can't be mostly honest or somewhat honest. We would operate with complete honesty and rectify whenever a mistake was made or the customer made an oversight in our favor. It didn't mean we didn't make mistakes or get things wrong; it just meant we would rectify any error that was identified.

The key to these core values being effective was twofold:

1. They were communicated both in content and expectation.
2. We followed them ourselves without wavering.

Now back to the rub. If you find your situation to be such that one of these two is not fully implemented, then you will have a hard time expecting your team to uphold those core values with any level of commitment.

If it is number one, then the path forward is clear and concise. Communicate the content of the core values and expectations for the team to uphold—repeatedly. In business meetings, in newsletters, on posters, on mouse pads, on notepads, and wherever else it makes sense to do so, communicate the M/V/CV.

If it is number two, then the path forward will be a little bit more challenging. You will have to assess where you are committed to the core values and where you are wavering from them. The problem stems from the fact that while you may be struggling with only one value, those watching you will lump them all together and say that since you don't follow all of them, none of them are really that important. It's a tough spot to be in but not insurmountable.

Recently, I found myself in a peculiar situation, going from a business owner for fifteen years to becoming an employee of a midsize company. As a business owner, I had full authority to establish the characteristics of the company and what would be the drivers of our reputation. We had created the core values, established their meaning, and pushed the team to live up to them. Now I had to follow the guidelines established by someone else.

This is a difficult struggle for an entrepreneur but one I came to realize had tremendous impact. I was on stage, and if I pushed back against something, my team would follow suit. I had to embrace the new core values as if I had created them. It is hard to change personal behavior, but when you realize the greater power of your influence by changing behavior, you can push through those challenges.

Self-commitment to uphold the company's mission / vision / core values is a powerful source of energy and growth for an individual. Not only do your direct reports see your behavior, but those in leadership above see it as well. Consistency is again the key. Live these principles out loud and see the ripple effect that flows through the performance of your team. When your team realizes you are fully committed to the M/V/CV, they will respond with similar commitment and potentially boost their energy and passion toward meeting those newly embraced values.

MEASURING COMMITMENT TO MISSION / VISION / CORE VALUES

Level 1

Doesn't see the need for, or value in connection to Mission/Vision/Core Values.

Level 2

Occasionally discusses the Mission/ Vision/Core Values in decision making.

Level 3

Sometimes connects decisions or communication to the Mission/Vision/ Core Values.

Level 4

Usually references some connection to Mission/Vision/Core Values in decision making and communication.

Level 5

Connects all activities and decision-making to mission / vision / core values and ensures others see the connection and value.

LEADERSHIP KEY #2:
MANAGING OTHERS

Good management consists in showing average
people how to do the work of superior people.
—John Rockefeller

MANAGING OTHERS

One of the most challenging transitions in an individual's career is the shift to a supervisor or manager. Just when you have mastered your own behavior at an acceptable level, you get thrown into the forays of helping others harness their inner greatness—sometimes whether they want you to or not.

How we manage ourselves and how we manage others is the guiding path toward great leadership. How we handle those two opportunities gives us the platform to earn the honor of having people follow us. Otherwise, they only do what we tell them as their superior. John Maxwell refers to this as "positional authority," the lowest level of leadership. There is a distinct difference between managing and leading, but they are very connected. You can manage people and not lead them. You will very seldom be able to lead people if you don't also manage them well.

Over the next few pages, we will look at some of the key characteristics needed to manage people well. Effective management is fundamental to high performance. It is also a key to maintaining a stable work environment and workforce. Statistics show that most people leave their position due to their direct supervisor or manager, not for more money or better benefits. An *Inc.* magazine study showed that "employees who rate their supervisor's performance poorly are four times as likely to be job hunting."

There is very little glamour or fanfare created from the results of managing effectively. I mean, when was the last great movie about an above-average manager? The stories are always about the great leader, the dynamic persona, but if we look closely, we can see that before there was great leadership, there was effective managing. We all strive to have consistently high-performing teams under our lead, so let's dive into the second group of stepping-stones to great leadership.

COMMUNICATION

Communication is an *exchange* of information from both the sender and the receiver. The US military provides a great standard and explanation of how this should be done through their radio communication protocol. Here is the expectation pulled from an excerpt on military English (Stanag6001.com):

> Use "CLEAR", "OVER", "OUT" when you finish your message. It notifies the addressee that you finished your portion of information and wait for the response or just ended the transmission ("OUT" word).

> When you have understood the message, acknowledge the receipt with the words "COPY", "RECEIVED", "ROGER" or "ACKNOWLEDGED." The word "COPY" is preferred.

While our day-to-day communication might not need the sharpness and accuracy required by the military, this example provides clarity about what an exchange of information can look like.

One of the special things we did as an organization was to conduct town hall meetings with our team members across the country. Since we had team members performing work in more than one hundred locations on a daily basis, we had to conduct a number of town hall meetings in order to get in front of as many team members as possible. The town hall was a great tool to share where the company was currently, reinforce the mission / vision / core values focus, and share where we were going as a team. Additionally, the town hall meetings provided a platform for the team to ask questions and speak directly with management and support functions that were typically only available if there was a crisis or major issue.

Inevitably, one of the takeaways from our town hall meetings was a need to improve communication. Mostly it involved the lack of information cascading down from management through the various levels of supervision. Poor communication results in blanks in the story that get filled in by the individual with whatever fears or concerns they have at the moment. A lack of clear communication is a major contributor to the potentially damaging rumor mill.

Nothing frustrated me more than to hear one of my managers reply to a question about whether or not they communicated a topic to the appropriate team with a response of "Well, I sent out an email with all of the details." While email is the most common form of sharing information, it is a horrible tool for effective communication. As mentioned earlier, communication is an *exchange* of information from both the sender and the receiver. The key word in that definition is the word exchange—a giving and receiving process. Unless there was a confirmation message back from the receiver, there is no exchange.

Exchange a business card with a new contact, and what happens? You give one, and you get one. Effective communication ensures there is an exchange on both ends. Confirm receipt and answer any questions that may exist from the information provided.

***Communication is an exchange of information
between both the sender and the receiver.***

Understanding your audience is another key element of effective communication. We are in the midst of the greatest transition of workforce from one generation to the next, or in this case to the next-next generation. Baby boomers were the largest component of the workforce over the past twenty years, accounting for more than 50 percent of the labor pool at one time. Generation X has held about a 30 percent position in the workforce. Millennials have been on a rapid increase in overall work population since the early 2000s and in 2017 became the largest group in the workforce. This trend is expected to continue over the next ten years as boomers exit the workforce (Pew Research 2017).

Significant study has shown there are distinct differences in how the population of the different working groups communicate. See the chart below that outlines some of the key differences in these groups.

	Baby Boomers	Gen X	Millennials
Communication	Face-to-Face	Immediate and direct	Email or texting
Work Attitude	Loyal to the job	Works to live	Play and work
Information	Prefer hard copy	Electronic copy	Shared file review
Work Expectations	Respect the title	Respect my ideas	Respect my time
Focus	On process	On results	On involvement
Priorities	Work comes first	Family comes first	Friends come first

While not everyone in these groups necessarily adopts to the premise listed in the chart, the tendencies have proven out over time and analysis. Use the information to see how best to communicate with the different work groups on your team.

Another key area of understanding is the techniques we utilize in communicating our message. While there are many media means to share our information, there is no substitute for face-to-face interaction. It is very challenging to inflect passion and emphasis in text messages or other written media. Additionally, *Psychology Today* breaks down the effectiveness of expression into three categories: actual words, tone, and nonverbal clues.

Their studies show that the receiver of your communication is assessing the information at the following rate:

➢   55 percent nonverbal
➢   38 percent tone
➢   7 percent actual words

With this data in mind, any information in written form is only 7 percent effective in actual communication. A conference call is only 45 percent effective. We have a digital and scattered workforce, so I understand the reality of how we have to communicate, but keep in mind that due to the structure of your team, you may need to increase the number of times you communicate things to achieve full absorption.

Last thing to remember is to overcommunicate. It is the old Dale Carnegie adage: Tell them what you are going to tell them, tell them, and tell them what you told them. And then tell them again. Very rarely will you be told to tone it back on the communication thing already!

Effective and consistent communication is a key step to building a great team and positioning yourself as a sound leader. Giving praise is a valuable aspect of good communication, as we will discuss in the next chapter.

MEASURING HOW OUR TEAM WOULD RATE OUR LEVEL OF PROPER COMMUNICATION

Level 1

Have unclear expectations and are provided little feedback on performance.

Level 2

On occasion my manager reviews the performance of me and my peers and provides feedback.

Level 3

Inconsistent communication from my manager; sometimes have good feedback and clarity on expectations, other times very little.

Level 4

Usually have clear understanding of expectations and current performance.

Level 5

Almost always know where we stand regarding expectations and performance.

PRAISE

Good job. Thanks for staying over. I appreciate your attention to the details. You have a great attitude.

Two of our primary management responsibilities are time and money. We want to spend as little money as possible and apply the least amount of time to complete the task. Efficiency is key. We are always on the lookout for tools to help drive efficiency. Whole industries are in place to help us find the right ways to move forward with gains in cost and timing. Getting more productivity and output with the people and resources we currently have is the constant ask from our executives.

People who feel appreciated are likely to stay longer, work harder, and contribute more than those who feel unappreciated. William James, early American psychologist and philosopher, states the following: "The deepest principle of human nature is a craving to be appreciated."

Praise is one of the most effective and efficient tools in our toolbox. The beauty of praise, in a nutshell, is that it doesn't cost us anything to give and takes very little time to deliver. All we have to do is take the time to recognize the moments and deliver the praise.

Gracious words are a honeycomb, sweet to the soul and healing to the bones.
—Proverbs 16:24 (NIV)

One of my managers was going through a very rough patch with his leadership group. He was responsible for the operations at several manufacturing locations, and there just seemed to be issue after issue happening at each location. His demeanor and countenance were obviously a bit downtrodden due to the continued troubles he had to maneuver through each week. Our company has an annual awards banquet where the top performing branches and profit centers are recognized for their performance the previous year. This manager was there to celebrate with one of the locations he managed that had qualified for the event.

A particular award is given each year to an individual who is nominated by their subordinates for the Manager of the Year and selected by the corporate committee. This manager was nominated, and he ultimately was selected by the committee to be recognized as the Manager of the Year. Afterward, he shared with us how this recognition had really been a boost for his morale. He was feeling very weary of the ongoing struggles, but this award, this praise, provided a significant jolt to his outlook.

While we can't give a Manager of the Year award out to everyone, there are always opportunities to recognize people for their contributions and efforts. Praise is a great tool for keeping a positive work environment and helps to keep motivated people motivated.

From Homebase: Nine Ways to Praise Your Employees

1. Match the praise to the effort.
2. Write a sincere thank-you note.
3. Remember their anniversary date.
4. Go public.
5. Give mini gifts.
6. Go behind the scenes.
7. Be surprising.
8. Award special assignments.
9. Be specific.

From *Inc.* magazine: Nine Elements of Highly Effective Praise

1. Don't wait.
2. Be specific.
3. Be genuine.
4. Save constructive feedback for later.
5. Go hunting (for opportunities to praise).
6. Be surprising (unexpected gifts/praise).
7. Strike a balance (with performers).
8. Create a recognition culture.
9. Treat employees like snowflakes.

If you find yourself in a season where you simply do not provide much praise to those around you, take a look at your thankfulness balance sheet. Praise that is genuine comes from a thankful heart. We will talk about being genuine as it relates to inspiring others later, but it is connected to the topic of praise and humility. When we look at what we have and appreciate those people and things rather than what we don't have, our outlook and attitude can shift toward gratitude rather than disgruntled.

The continuing value of praising employees is also a multiplier effect. If you are continually finding opportunities to praise your top leaders, they will tend to do the same thing. With a little prodding, you can probably help them establish this as a habit. Ultimately, the habits of the team become the culture of the team. Recognition and praise are simple, inexpensive elements for building high-performing teams and should be a part of any strong leader's management strategy.

MEASURING OUR TEAM'S ASSESSMENT REGARDING GIVING PRAISE

Level 1

I only get feedback on what I do wrong.

Level 2

Seldom get recognition for exceptional performance and it is done in private.

Level 3

Occasionally get recognized for outstanding performance and in a public setting.

Level 4

Manager typically recognizes top performance and points out behaviors that make the team excellent.

Level 5

Manager makes individuals feel valued and recognized for their contributions to the team.

TEAM BUILDING

The total is greater than the sum of all parts. We can accomplish more together than we can individually. Teams provide perspective and clarity of purpose and help maintain performance expectations.

As managers, we need to create an environment that promotes interaction and interdependence with the team members, driving performance to company goals and helping individuals achieve their own goals. Not so complicated and sounds pretty easy, right? Well, not so much.

The power of team is almost immeasurable. Year after year, we see sports teams with less talent but great team chemistry win championships. What makes one team perform at such high levels while others seem to only get glimpses of greatness when it comes to teamwork?

Tony Dungy reflected on his time at the Indianapolis Colts in his book *Quiet Strength* by saying this: "My challenge with the Colts was to sell them on the idea that teams win championships. We needed to come together as a complete team-offense, defense and special teams." Dungy took over the Colts in 2002 and proceeded to lead the team to nine consecutive playoff appearances, winning the Super Bowl in 2006 and losing to the Saints in the Super Bowl in 2009.

Another great reflection of Coach Dungy's approach to team building was in the response from star quarterback Peyton Manning: "Coach, I'm glad you're here. I want to be coached. I want to win. I want you to treat me like any other player and teach me what I need to do because I want to win." Dungy created an environment where even the top performers were willing to do what was necessary for the whole team to win.

We needed to come together as a complete team.
—Tony Dungy

When individuals are willing to sacrifice time, effort, and energy to work through those tasks or duties that are mundane and irritating on behalf of others on their team, great things can happen. One sacrifice leads to another. One commitment drives a second and a third. Now the momentum can build within the unit to do more together than would have ever been possible separately.

So how do we create a team environment as a leader? A great question, without a simple answer or a three-step process. There are, however, some realistic steps we can take to help promote the type of environment necessary to generate a strong team environment.

First and foremost is to build trust. Teamwork can rarely exist or flourish without the basis of trust among the team members. Trust allows for individuals to become vulnerable (emotionally) with one another with the belief that the other person will treat the responsibility of that access with respect. When someone becomes vulnerable, they open themselves up for both positive and negative feedback from their peers.

The ultimate level of satisfaction as a manager is realizing that the team under your leadership is providing their own level of accountability within the group, without your prodding or intervention. Self-policing regarding policies and performance expectations within a team is a strong indicator of a team approaching hyper performance potential.

The Golden State Warriors provide a glimpse of a hyper-performing team that has the appearance of a self-managed group of people. Steve Kerr, head coach for the Warriors, is often heard during time-out conversations talking about the emotional side of performance: attitude, effort, and trust. The teammates are seen discussing with one another the tactical adjustments that need to be made. When an individual doesn't put forth the effort that should be given, the teammates call them out, not Coach Kerr. In fact, during an unusual losing streak, Kerr handed the reins over to players to coach themselves through the difficulty. The players embraced the opportunity, and the losing streak quickly came to a halt.

The results of this are obvious, with Golden State winning the NBA title in three of the past four seasons (2015–2018) and losing in the finals to Lebron James and the Cleveland Cavaliers in the other season. So, Kerr has been to the finals in each of the four seasons he has coached. A pretty impressive run and an outstanding example of what is possible when we create a flourishing team environment.

A team is not a group of people who work together. A team is a group of people who trust each other.
—Simon Sinek

The benefits of building a top-performing team are endless, and it is usually the primary responsibility of the manager to facilitate it. While each individual has to make the decision to become vulnerable to the other team members, as managers, we create the environment that supports the openness and trust needed. Point your efforts toward building the proper environment that protects trust and openness and see what great things your team can accomplish.

MEASURING OUR TEAM'S PERCEPTION ON TEAM BUILDING

Level 1

> Manager is clearly focused on their own professional growth rather than that of the team.

Level 2

> Manager typically focus on individual performance to metrics with little discussion about team performance.

Level 3

> Manager provides some dialogue about individual performance and the link to the overall team's performance.

Level 4

> Manager's primary focus is around team dynamics and team performance.

Level 5

> Manager is focused on building a cohesive unit that is continually getting better as individuals and as a group.

TEACH AND COACH

We all have opportunity to influence others to achieve great things, both personally and professionally. While we will have more influence with some people than others, there is still an opportunity for us to help people on their journey through life. There is no greater joy than to see a team member accomplish something they have been working toward for some time. Accepting a new promotion, completing continuing studies, or hitting a milestone in a performance plan are accomplishments we can help our team members achieve.

As a former coach of world-class basketball players (okay, maybe not world-class but high-energy preteen girls) for nine years and high school boys for the past four years, I have had the pleasure of working with varying degrees of skill and confidence among my players. I had one boy that played for me who realized his capabilities during the season. Jack was a freshman and had been blessed with a height deficiency. He had sufficient skills in dribbling, passing, and shooting along with decent quickness, and during practice scrimmages with his teammates, he would play relaxed and confidently.

Whenever we played in a real game, however, Jack would start to play hot potato rather than basketball. It seemed that once he got the ball in his hands, his only mission was to get it to someone else as quickly as possible. He was demonstrating a definitive fear of failure by his play.

During a break in the action of one game in particular, Jack had received a pass and stood alone by the three-point line and failed to take the shot. As he came to the bench, I made direct eye contact and told him to shoot it. As the break ended, I pulled Jack aside and challenged him with this statement: "Jack, you have the ability to perform and can make baskets for the team. When you don't shoot, you are actually being more selfish by not taking any chances and hurting your teammates. If you are not going to shoot it, then I will need to replace you with someone else who will take a chance for the benefit of the team."

During the next series of plays, Jack got another opportunity with the ball in hand and wide-open space between him and the defenders. This time, he looked to the basket, loaded, and fired a shot from beyond the three-point line. I don't remember if it was nothing but net, but it went in the hoop with confidence. Jack's expression of joy and excitement was instant and full. Hands in the air, he bounced down the court to teammates just as thrilled as he was to celebrate with him as he crossed midcourt. Jack didn't make all of his shots, but he became a more valuable team member and a more confident young man in the process.

Similar to Jack, we have to sometimes coach our team members to realize the alternate views of decisions and situations. It is human nature to look at things from a personal, selfish perspective. As managers, we have to teach our team, especially the potential future leaders, the value of a broader perspective. What if everyone on the team took the same view as Jack and no one was willing to take a shot? It's hard to win at anything if you are not willing to risk failing.

Many of the other fundamental building blocks of effective management are learned through the help of coaches and teachers: time management, business acumen, and many others.

**Give a man a fish and you feed him for a day. Teach
a man to fish and you feed him for a lifetime.
—Chinese proverb**

The challenge is in balancing the control side of things to make sure the tasks needed to be completed are done properly while developing the individuals so that over time it requires less and less of your input. As I mentioned earlier in this chapter, we all have influence over those in our circle, both under our management and outside of our management.

Raising children is a great example of balancing control and influence. When children are younger, your attention is much more associated with controlling the environments and actions due to their lack of understanding and decision-making skills. As the children grow in knowledge and experience, they require less and less control and influence to make proper choices.

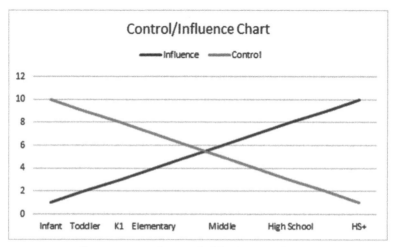

Concept visual provided by Dewey Greene

Our team member's growth and development is similar to that of a child's. We have to provide clarity and expectations regarding their direct behavior in the beginning, but as their knowledge and understanding of what is expected grows, we lessen our focus on control and shift to influence. Teaching and coaching are the targeted investment of time and knowledge to those under our care and direction. The better we approach this responsibility, the more benefits we will gain from a maturing team.

Another way to look at this segment is how proficient a manager is at getting the team ready to manage themselves. We often assess coaches by two factors:

- their personal win/loss performance
- their coaching lineage created

Bill Walsh, former coach of the San Francisco 49ers from 1979 to 1988, changed the strategies utilized in the NFL and won three championships during his tenure. Additionally, Walsh had five of his coaches go on to become head coaches in the NFL. Mike Holmgren was one of those coaches who also had five of his coaches become head coaches. In total, Walsh is responsible for developing twenty-seven head coaches in the NFL by his teaching and coaching.

As we assess our impact in our organization, we need to make the long-term influence of being a manager one of the key metrics we strive to impact. The more we focus on influencing instead of controlling, the more likely we are to create future managers and leaders for our organization.

MEASURING OUR TEAM'S IMPRESSION ON TEACHING AND COACHING

Level 1

Manager spends very little time providing perspective and instruction on how better to do things.

Level 2

Team seldom experiences or witnesses skill development sessions from the manager.

Level 3

Manager takes some time to help individuals in one area or another.

Level 4

Manager is often helping team members assess their skills and growth strategies.

Level 5

Manager makes it a priority to spend significant time with individuals to broaden their thought processes and demonstrate improvement methods.

ACCOUNTABLE

One of the most challenging functions of a manager is to hold themselves and their team accountable for performance. It is especially difficult for someone who has transitioned from colleague to supervisor or manager over the same group they used to work with.

The biggest contributor to this accountability struggle is ambiguity—that is, the lack of clear definition of what is expected behavior and how the behavior will be measured. For many organizations, the results expected are often clearly defined, but the behaviors of the team to obtain those results are usually as clear as mud, or the Hudson River, if you live in NY. In either comparison, the truth is that without clarity about behavioral performance expectations, the opportunity for poor accountability is introduced into the working relationship.

Initially, a manager must establish their own behavioral boundaries and expectations in managing a group of people to accomplish the defined metrics. If goals and expectations are not clearly established, it will be very challenging to hold people accountable to an unknown metric. We discuss goal-setting techniques a little later, so take time now to clarify the metrics that are critical to performance so that holding people accountable is realistic and reasonable.

As a manager, we are always on stage when it comes to behavior and performance. The best predictor of a strong performing team is a strong performing manager. Bringing a positive attitude to work, being on time for phone or in-person meetings, communicating with respect at all times, completing projects with excellence, and doing what you say you will do are some key behaviors a leader can adhere to as an example for their team. The "Managing Yourself" section of the book outlines more key aspects of self-management and performance.

Once the personal behavioral boundaries are established, the manager can focus on establishing expectations for their team. Focus on what is most important for the team dynamic and the performance metrics the team is expected to deliver. If you are in a manufacturing plant setting and being on time to morning meetings is important to set the priority for the day's production, establish that as a priority. If the team works remotely most of the time, that metric would seem authoritarian and potentially unreasonable. The second group, however, could be accountable to update a progress tracker prior to the weekly conference call. Every team dynamic is unique, and the thoughtful manager will engage the team to establish those boundaries for behavioral performance.

When Chuck Daly was introduced as the coach for the US Basketball Dream Team in the 1992 Olympic Games, he could have made any number of demands or requests to the players, but he chose to focus on just one priority. Be on time. Out of respect for fellow teammates, be on time for meetings, for the bus, and for practices. Remember, this was a group that included Michael Jordan, Charles Barkley, John Stockton, Larry Bird, Karl Malone, and other Hall of Fame players of the day. He recognized the dynamic of this group and focused on what he believed to be the key element of behavior that would help the team be successful at what mattered most, winning the gold medal. The players would later reveal that even Charles Barkley was on time for everything! The result was a dominant march to the gold medal by this incredible assembly of players. Coach Daly had identified the key attribute that would help this group come together to be successful: respect for one another.

The next key step is to establish a consistent model for acknowledging adherence to the behavioral standards or noncompliance. Consistency is the key. What we learn from human nature is if we don't get feedback on our behavior, we tend to push the boundaries until we get the feedback. Our team's behavior is not what we ask for or write down on a behavior statement. Our team's behavior is typically what we tolerate. So, if being on time for meetings is deemed an important behavior, then when one of the members is late for the meeting, the leader must address the behavior as unsatisfactory.

Typically, when the behavior is confirmed to be important by the manager, the team will begin to self-manage to that standard. The ideal operating standard for a team is when the goals and metrics are clearly established, the behavior expectations are firmly set, and the team is monitoring its own behavior to those established expectations. When this level of team commitment is achieved, the manager is free to focus on leadership development, continuous improvement, or even new responsibilities to take on with the team.

A key item to remember about accountability is the fact that accountability cannot be transferred to another member of the team. As the manager, you are responsible for the team's behavior and performance. You can transfer responsibility for some things to get completed, but accountability for the outcome still falls on the shoulder of the manager.

I liken this to a scenario I often experienced with my children as they were growing up. I would ask one of the kids to empty the dishwasher as one of their chores and find out later that it wasn't completed. When I would go back to the child and ask about the dishwasher not being emptied, they would reply that they told one of the other siblings to do it. While that would be fine if the work had been completed, I explained that they were accountable to make sure that the dishwasher was emptied, regardless of who they asked to help them complete the task.

> *Our team's performance is not what we ask for or write down on a behavior statement; our team's performance is typically what we tolerate.*

Providing a clear expectation and accountability process is a fundamental component of team development. As each member demonstrates their comprehension of the expectations and deliverables associated with their function, they are then ready to take on additional responsibilities. This cycle of expectation, accountability, and delegation provides the framework for individual growth and development as well as team growth.

MEASURING OUR TEAM'S IMPRESSION ON ACCOUNTABILITY

Level 1

Manager allows some individuals to have a "free pass" when it comes to performance while holding others to a specific standard.

Level 2

Manager sometimes holds the team to a standard but usually just wings it.

Level 3

Manager usually keeps track of all performance but sometimes doesn't hold people accountable to the standard.

Level 4

Manager typically reviews performance of each individual to the expected outcomes.

Level 5

Manager holds all team members to the expected performance and behavioral standards.

MOTIVATE

Growing up as an athlete, I experienced different types of motivation from different coaches and mentors. There was the intimidating coach who tried to make me perform with a "do this or else" approach. Then I also had the encouraging type of coach who was primarily a big cheerleader to me. He would make statements like "You can do this" or "You got this" to spur my emotions toward completion or learning the assignment. There were still others who pushed the pride button and would say things like "I thought you were better than that, but I guess not" or "You probably won't be able to get this" as a tool to drive me to prove them wrong.

All of these approaches have a place in our strategy as leaders as we determine what buttons have an impact on our team. What causes an individual to respond and grow, to be willing to sacrifice to get better or achieve a better outcome? Some folks are eager to respond to someone in their face, challenging them to do more. For others, this approach would cause them to withdraw from the moment and potentially from the process altogether.

We can't use just one approach to motivate those who work for us or those we are empowered to influence. A key thing to remember about human nature is that we tend to use the method we are most comfortable receiving as our primary method of motivating. Understanding this about ourselves is fundamental to learning how to approach each team member and get the most out of the talent we have been given the opportunity to grow. Great managers learn the balance of influence and control to reach the pinnacle of motivational impact.

I had a football coach in high school who shared a story of one of his players from years earlier in his coaching career. This particular player was an undersized defensive lineman who wasn't particularly a gifted athlete but had good skills and a passionate desire to perform. The next opponent for the team had an offensive lineman who was garnering state recognition for his performance and was a large, gifted athlete.

All through the week of preparation, the coach would tell his defensive lineman that his opponent was talented and gifted, but he didn't believe that the opposing player would have any success blocking him that week. He challenged the lineman to work hard and see that he was better than the other guy. He was hungrier. He was quicker. He was smarter. Every day, he poured into this lineman the idea that he could outplay the superstar from the opponent's team.

On that Friday night, the undersized, less talented defensive lineman wreaked havoc on the offense, consistently beating the highly touted offensive player. Coach remembers this story because it is a reminder of the power of motivation.

A key element of motivation is having a defined goal to accomplish and driving the team's performance and behaviors to accomplish the goal. In sports, the goal is relatively easy to define, as in most cases it is to win the game or event in which you are competing. In business, the goal sometimes is less obvious, especially if you work for a large organization. Helping to define goals that are meaningful to the individual performer is critical.

> *Coach remembers this story because it is a*
> *reminder of the power of motivation.*

Utilizing the SMART goal-setting technique is a straightforward method for establishing what will be important to measure:

Specific
Measurable
Achievable

Relevant
Time-Bound

Establishing goals for our team to accomplish gives us specific objectives so we can push and motivate our team to accomplish more than they think is possible.

Once the goals are established, the next step is learning the motivation buttons for each of our team members. Obtaining this information can be a challenge, as it takes time that may appear to be noncore to the management function. My experience tells me quite the opposite is true.

Knowing how to communicate the goals and desired outcomes expected in a clear and concise manner, in different motivational languages, is a powerful tool for building high-performing teams.

Keep it simple. Measure regularly. Motivate specifically.

MEASURING OUR TEAM'S VIEW ON MOTIVATION

Level 1

I only hear from my manager when expectations are not met.

Level 2

Seldom hear words of encouragement or support for ongoing growth and development.

Level 3

Sometimes receive encouragement to perform or reach higher, but mostly just assess the current performance.

Level 4

Manager recognizes most of the time when I am not giving my best and challenges me to do better.

Level 5

Manager understands my goals and aspirations and encourages me to push toward my potential.

CARE

You are probably familiar with the quote credited to Theodore Roosevelt: "Nobody cares how much you know until they know how much you care."

Caring is perhaps one of the most challenging aspects of managing, as it is not a readily visible aspect of the job, such as attendance or safety or quality metrics. Additionally, how people feel cared for is as varied as the sky on a beautiful sunrise. Each day is different, and each person's feeling of being cared for can be as fluid as the clouds flowing across a morning sky.

That being said, a person who feels cared for will typically outperform someone who doesn't feel it, will stay working for the company longer, foregoing better offers of pay and benefits, and will typically do better quality work than their uncared-for counterparts. The benefits of delivering a cared-for feeling to our teams are critically important for lasting success.

The leaders who get the most out of their people are the leaders who care most about their people.
—Simon Sinek

The initial hurdle to overcome when it relates to caring is the fact that it is, in actuality, a feeling. Just like loyalty and commitment, care comes from emotion. The key is to understand how to connect the emotion of care with each of our team members. Perhaps the best first step is to establish a genuine interest in them as individuals. Know their families, their hobbies, and their volunteer outlets. Know them.

One of the next ways to make a caring connection is to find out how best the individual receives appreciation and love. Just like motivation, we tend to give out recognition and love the way we like to receive it from others. Just by finding out what a team member's love language (*The Five Love Languages*, Gary Chapman) preference is we make a lasting connection with them. Taking the time to understand them as an individual is an expression of taking care of them.

For example, one employee may benefit the most from a public acknowledgment and appreciation of a job well done (affirmation), while another employee would much rather receive a small plaque recognizing an accomplishment (gifts). Each person is unique, and knowing how they best receive care from us is a powerful connecting point. The other languages outlined in *The Five Love Languages* are (1) time together, (2) touch, and (3) acts of service.

Additionally, caring for our team members means understanding that life is not lived in compartments but that their work life and their home life are intertwined and interconnected. While our expectation is for their home life not to interfere with their work accomplishments, we demonstrate an understanding of the influence home life can have. Just listening to what might be happening with their kids or spouse or aging parents or a myriad of other potential life issues provides a feeling of security and safety for them. Displaying empathy for the situation and offering ways to support them through their trial builds loyalty and commitment levels that are hard to measure but are rewarded through unwavering dedication and loyalty.

Additionally, *People* magazine's "Companies That Care" list for 2018 noted that people who experience a caring workplace are 44 percent more likely to be a part of company with above-average revenue growth. So, caring is not just touchy-feely mumbo jumbo; it creates an environment of trust and performance that is reflected through employee engagement and productivity.

MEASURING OUR TEAM'S FEELING OF CARE

Level 1

Manager doesn't express genuine concern about the individual, only about the results.

Level 2

Manager will occasionally reflect on personal impact of the business.

Level 3

Manager reflects empathy in communication, but the emphasis is still primarily on the results.

Level 4

Manager balances the impact of business and the personal interaction in most dialogue and circumstances.

Level 5

Manager demonstrates genuine concern for the person and not just for the output.

POLICIES MANAGEMENT

One of the biggest areas of concern I have experienced and witnessed during my time in large and small organizations is the topic of balanced policy management of subordinates. Nothing stirs the emotions like feeling you have been treated more harshly than a coworker for the same offense. As we have mentioned before, managers are always on stage and never more so than in this area of policy enforcement.

Let me build a scenario to demonstrate the key point in this category. John, a young manager in the engineering department, is an avid golfer and often competes in tournaments with one of his subordinates, Ben, on the weekends. They have trophies on their desks proclaiming their golfing prowess and comradery for all to see. What others see is a close relationship between John and Ben. Others keep a careful eye on how the rules apply to Ben versus everyone else. Over time, you begin to see Ben showing up a little late on Mondays after a long weekend of golfing. The team notices that John seems to turn the other way or react as if Ben were arriving on time like the rest of the team. What the team is experiencing is a breach of trust that everyone will be treated the same.

At first, it is just a few whispers of favoritism or jabs at how one or the other should pick up golf so they can get special treatment too. The undertow current has begun, and the novice manager will turn a deaf ear to the noise it creates. Usually a seasoned employee will take the time to let the young manager know about the noise and what they are hearing in the breakroom. Without an honest look at the situation, this scenario can end up in the HR department or even the legal department if the behavior is not leveled by upper management.

Nepotism, the policy of not having family members as direct reports, is a policy that organizations have to limit the special treatment that could be interpreted through these types of relationships. Close friendships between the boss and other coworkers can generate similar feelings of mistrust and unfairness. Feeling like you are being mistreated is a strong emotion, and strong emotions typically generate strong actions. Often these are what make it to the human resources desk as complaints.

A wise manager will do a self-check on how they are handling their team and will also seek counsel from one of their more senior team members or fellow managers for additional feedback. Once trust is broken in this area, it can be recovered, but it requires aggressive steps to distance the manager from the close subordinate. It is a lose-lose situation once you have reached this point, and you should take precautions to avoid this position.

While the process of handling the entire team with fairness and equal accountability to the policies can be straining, the end result is a team built on trust. Trust is the key element of high-performing teams, and this simple step of equal policy management helps develop that foundation of trust. Consistency in managing the team according to the policies and procedures is a must for growth as a manager and leader.

Trust is a key element of high-performing teams.

MEASURING ADMINISTRATION OF POLICIES AND PROCEDURES

Level 1

Manager shows favoritism or neglect in administering the policies.

Level 2

Manager is typically inconsistent in holding people accountable to the policies and procedures.

Level 3

Manager is sometimes inconsistent in execution to adherence to company policy requirements.

Level 4

Manager usually shows no favoritism to individuals regarding policy enforcement.

Level 5

Manager is fair and consistent in requiring compliance with policies and procedures.

LEADERSHIP KEY #3:
INSPIRE OTHERS

Our chief want is someone to inspire us to
be what we know we could be.
—Ralph Waldo Emerson

INSPIRE OTHERS

As mentioned earlier in the book, how we manage ourselves and how we manage others are the stepping-stones to being able to inspire others. We earn the chance to inspire others through the respect gained from effective management. Inspiring others brings fulfilment we should all hope to experience. Helping someone become something they do not believe is possible happens through the transformational power of inspiration!

There are a few people who reach a pinnacle of achievement and state that they knew from an early age they would be right at that point. For the vast majority, their first comment is usually "I can't believe I am here," followed by a list of people to thank. Almost every award ceremony is a demonstration of this scenario.

Somewhere along the journey, each individual was pushed to overcome obstacles or encouraged to ignore the naysayers. A small handful in our lives will tell us what they believe we can do and can become, but many will tell us what we can't do. Those who speak into our hearts to stay the course and not give up when things look the bleakest are the ones who end up on those lists. As leaders, we have a special opportunity to potentially land on an appreciation list.

We have the unique opportunity to look at our team members through multilayered lenses. By our position of authority, we are granted special influence over those team members who look up to us for acceptance, validation, and guidance. We can look through the lens of today and provide support for current accomplishments, and also look through the lens of tomorrow and instill the thoughts of what could be.

Taking the time to know each team member as an individual and to understand when to push and when to lift up helps establish the strong bonds that are reflected on during times of accomplishment. In this segment, we will focus on looking through the lens of what could be and see how our words and actions can help others achieve more than they ever believed possible.

There is little glamour and glitz in managing ourselves well and managing others well, but by inspiring others, we can reap rewards of accomplishment we could never attain ourselves. It is in this phase that we climb the leadership ladder and begin to approach what John Maxwell lists at Level 4 (Reproduction) and Level 5 (Respect) of leadership recognition. These levels take time and significant effort and focus, but the journey to becoming a legacy leader is realized through the inspiration of others.

OTHERS FIRST

When leaders put their team members first, the response from the team is a commitment and zeal that is not realized through any other means. Our objective is to create an environment where our team feels safe and empowered to do their work to the best of their ability. This means taking care of them before taking care of ourselves.

In the early days of EHD Technologies, we had a few employees that we hired to help provide the engineering support requested from our clients. As we approached the Christmas season, we wanted to recognize the efforts and contributions made by these employees to help solidify our brand in the marketplace. As any small business owner will tell you, cash is king, and we had experienced good growth the previous year, which consumed our available cash. My partner and I decided it would be best to still pay our team a bonus even though it meant we would not take any money out ourselves. The impact of this decision built a level of loyalty and trust from our employees that carried us from that point to our next growth level.

From a tactical perspective, as a leader, we need to keep our team focused on the ultimate goal as it applies to our business objectives, and simultaneously help each team member accomplish their individual goals. A phrase I often use is this: "If I help you accomplish what you want to accomplish and get you where you want to go, then I will get where I want to go as well."

This statement assumes the individual's goals are in alignment with the broader goals of the team. For example, if one of my sales team wants to reach a new commission level and I can assist them in modifying their planning and sales execution to accomplish it, we both benefit from them hitting their goal.

Think about it. What will motivate an individual more? Meeting their own goals or meeting my goals? Obviously, meeting their own goals will deliver much more motivation. That being said, our primary responsibility is to establish the broader goals for the team, but closely behind that responsibility is the need to understand the personal goals of our team members.

> **You can get everything in life you want if you will just**
> **help enough other people get what they want.**
> **—Zig Ziglar**

Sports demonstrate the characteristics of solid teamwork and provide relatable visuals for business application. There are early mornings and long days to complete the tasks on time and to meet the objectives set forth for the team to accomplish. When the time comes for the championship moment and the team is victorious, what is the scenario we often see in sports? The players carry the coach off the field on their shoulders. The culmination of excitement and joy in the accomplishment is a recognition of the role the leader played in bringing the group to that point.

Just like in sports, we work countless hours with our team members through good times and bad. While being carried out of the conference room is not a likely scenario in an office setting, the potential celebration from your team can be similar to those enjoyed by the winning coaches. Our hope is to receive praise and respect for helping the group accomplish their goals.

If we can help align each team member's activities and growth with the goals and objectives of the entire team, we create an opportunity for celebration when the group accomplishes the outlined targets. When we focus on the goals of others first, we build not only credibility but also trust and loyalty that drives continuing motivation and performance from our team members.

Putting others' desires ahead of our own aspirations is a stepping-stone to achieving lasting impact and provides the foundation for us to help inspire our team to achieve even greater things.

MEASURING HOW WELL WE PUT OTHERS FIRST

Level 1

Manager seldom inquires or assesses the impact of circumstances to team members.

Level 2

Manager usually assesses the impact to their own aspirations rather than the impact to the team members.

Level 3

Manager is inconsistent in monitoring team goals over personal goals.

Level 4

Manager tends to look at the impact to the team as a first view, but sometimes still assesses from a personal impact first.

Level 5

Exemplifies helping the team get what they need before fulfilling personal objectives.

INSPIRE

Each person is unique and processes their opinions about their skills, experience, and potential differently. Some people tend to maximize the impact and limitations of their flaws in comparing their skills, talents, and experiences to those of others. Others tend to overlook their own shortcomings and focus on the limitations of others.

There has been extensive study about how differently men and women look at themselves and the impact on their potential. In her book *The Secret Thoughts of Successful Women*, Valerie Young discusses the impact of what she calls the Imposter Syndrome:

> A shocking number of accomplished women in all career paths and at every level feel as though they are faking it—imposters in their own lives and careers ... "It's only because they like me. I was in the right place at the right time. I just work harder than the others. I don't deserve this. It's just a matter of time before I am found out."

A recent review of internal candidates at Hewlett-Packard revealed that men were willing to apply for a position if they met 60 percent of the qualifications, while women would apply only if they met 100 percent of the qualifications.

Understanding that each individual processes their own potential in different ways is a critical knowledge point for leaders to explore. Does the individual feel they lack experience, education, or a potential skill? Do they feel unqualified or unequal to the task, or do they just have a fear of failure? Our objective is to help each team member identify what is inhibiting their pursuit of goals and dreams. As leaders, we need to create an image of what is possible and what they can do to make their dreams a reality.

When you look at the varying definitions of the word *inspire*, there is one key element that stands out: inspiration is found from an external creative impulse or a breathed-in component. Personal willpower and self-inspiration play key roles in our long-term success, as we discuss later, but the vast majority of accomplishments occur through the inspirational efforts of someone other than ourselves.

Seeing someone we care about or have invested in achieve a dream or become inspired is one of the most rewarding aspects of living. As a parent, we aspire to raise our children to realize their potential, to dream big and accomplish more than they believe they can. We can treat our team members in a similar fashion, helping craft a path to success for each team member on their professional journey.

Ultimately, our goal is not to push them to be that person but for them to catch hold of the vision for themselves and commit to do the work to get there. While helping people grasp the purpose and necessity of the work on the path to accomplishment is when inspiration takes hold.

Very few great things are accomplished without the accompaniment of hard work. Ask any champion in sports or a successful businessperson about reaching that pinnacle, and they will tell you it all started when they went to work in the beginning. Either in preseason workouts or late-night work sessions, they became who they are through the process of hard work.

> **People miss out on opportunity because it is**
> **dressed in overalls and looks like work.**
> **—Ben Franklin**

The inspiring leader is there to encourage and challenge them through this season of hard work. There will be successes and failures during this work cycle, and being there to support individuals or teams through the struggle can provide the boost needed to overcome the obstacle.

An ironic twist to the impact we can have on them is that their ultimate goal may not be achieved while they are with us or our team. As we discussed in the "Others First" section, we have to see beyond our own needs and help people get to where they want to go. In so doing, we will build loyalty and dedication in our team. We will get the best effort out of those we are inspiring to accomplish their own dreams and goals.

Inspiring others with a genuine care for their aspirations may mean sacrificing focus on our goals for a season of time. The reward for maintaining this support and interest in others? Well, that's how you make the thank-you lists of those you inspired.

MEASURING OUR ABILITY TO INSPIRE

Level 1

> Manager tends to tear down ideas and aspirations of team members.

Level 2

> Manager seldom speaks of accomplishing greater things as a goal or objective for the team or individuals.

Level 3

> Manager sometimes delivers encouragement to pursue greater potential in team members.

Level 4

> Manager provides a steady outpouring of emotional energy to encourage the team to accomplish great things.

Level 5

> Manager is a constant supporter and driver of dreams and aspirations of each team member.

BUSINESS ACUMEN

Seeing the big picture is one of the most challenging transitions for individuals to make during their rise through the leadership ranks. People tend to continue to look at decision-making from their previous position's point of view and struggle to see the broader impact on the organization. Team decision-making can provide excellent perspective on how each part of the organization may be affected. While we can't always reach consensus, the more we understand the overall impact, the better decisions we will usually make.

The financial impact is a basic business lesson most aspiring young leaders need to learn, especially if they are a part of a larger organization. Even members of a smaller organization may not be exposed to the true financial indicators of the business, which are necessary to understand this topic. Rolling through the impact to gross margin and EBITDA, the fundamental drivers of all businesses, both for profit and nonprofit, is a powerful exercise every leader should provide for their team.

A year after our company was acquired, we were consolidating the commission plans from both organizations and identified some key performance indicators (KPIs) that we believed captured the important aspects of the varying positions within the commission plan.

For the sales team, we came up with items that they had a direct impact on during the sell process:

- gross margin percentage
- accounts receivable percentage past due

- gross margin to budget
- new accounts opened

For the operations team, we came up with items they had a direct impact on during the delivery process of our service:

- quality performance
- non-bill time
- gross margin to budget
- on-time reports to customers

There were several other KPIs that each group monitored on a weekly and monthly basis to maximize their commissions, and through this process, we found that the knowledge base for every group was greatly elevated due to them learning the impact of each KPI. For example, non-bill time was found to not only include hours that we had team members working that we could not bill the customer, but we also had another element that was driving up our non-bill time. What the team identified was whenever we had to pay one of our team members overtime and could only bill as straight time, it hit the metric negatively as well. The overall effect was each manager now understood what causes drove the KPI numbers, which in turn drove the profitability metrics as well. Sales and operations were able to adjust their focus on the topics that were hurting their team's overall performance.

While each business has unique characteristics and specialties, there are several areas that most organizations and leaders benefit from learning more about. Here are a few of those functions:

- the selling cycle
- project management
- technology
- quality control
- culture / mission / vision / core values
- human resources

- marketing
- data analytics

The more knowledge our leaders have, the better the decision-making process can be. Our goal should be for decisions to be made at the lowest levels possible. Nurturing the ability to make good judgments and quick decisions for the good of the company and all affected parties is a key objective for growing the team's capabilities.

The better equipped our leaders become, the more capable and ready they will be to step into new opportunities. Keeping the pipeline filled with growing leaders at every level is a key element of effective leadership. Twice per year, we hold business reviews with our teams, and one of the elements of the business review is identifying who the next leaders are and their development plans. These plans include expanding responsibilities, technical training, and soft skills training.

The better equipped our leaders become, the more capable and ready they will be to step into new opportunities.

Each member of our leadership team should be expanding their knowledge and understanding of what makes the business successful. We must continue to keep getting better and more efficient at what we do. We must keep climbing by reading, learning our business, and developing our leadership skills. You become who you spend time with and what you read. Never stop learning.

MEASURING OUR COMMITMENT TO GROWING BUSINESS ACUMEN IN OUR TEAM

Level 1

Manager doesn't share business knowledge and experience as a way to maintain superiority in the relationship.

Level 2

Manager tends to want to make most of the important decisions and does not challenge the team to grow in their decision-making skills.

Level 3

Manager instills some knowledge and experience to the team but does not prioritize expanding their knowledge base.

Level 4

Manager challenges the team to learn from others and expand their knowledge base and decision-making skills. Provides information to help facilitate the growth on many occasions

Level 5

Manager has tremendous knowledge and wisdom and is deliberate in sharing experiences with team members.

COMMUNICATION

As we discussed, communication is a fundamental and often underexecuted element of management. In the context of inspiring others, we shift our focus from the transfer of information to the sharing of philosophy and purpose.

Managing well requires clear objectives and tasks. Be on time. Make a hundred calls this week. Don't yell at the customers. Well, I hope the last one isn't on someone's task list, but you get the picture. To inspire people, we have to provide purpose and vision. We have to connect them to the bigger picture of what their day-to-day work means.

The big picture is also what drives one of the most important value propositions a leader can provide to their team: the why behind what we do and what we require our team to do. I would recommend the Simon Sinek book *Start with Why* as a great resource to explore this topic in greater detail if you do not have clarity on this key driver.

Providing a clear mission as to why the organization exists and a vision for where the organization is going are key elements to make sure they are viable and a part of ongoing conversations within the team. Additionally, having actionable core values established, communicated, and followed provides a solid foundation for predictable performance.

Tractor Supply Company TSCO (NASDAQ), headquartered in Brentwood, Tennessee, provides a tremendous example of how effectively defining the mission and core values of the organization can be accomplished. In fact, the headquarters isn't even called headquarters. It is called the Store Support Center. Talk about strong communication and establishing expectations for all who work there! The message is loud and clear that their purpose is to support the operation and success of their stores.

Tractor Supply has more than 1,750 stores located in forty-nine states in the US and has more than 29,000 employees (as of the end of 2018). I had an opportunity to interact with the current CEO, Greg Sandfort, and learn how they have built their company culture so effectively. Greg quickly acclaimed his predecessors, Jim Wright and Joe Scarlett, for laying the foundation and then pulled out the laminated card that he carried with him all the time.

On the card are listed the mission and values of the organization. You can go to their website at tractorsupply.com/mission-and-values to review them. Every team member's security badge has these printed on them. They are printed in large banners and on wall art when you enter the Support Center. They are in conference rooms and break rooms. They are discussed in meetings and in planning sessions. The mission and values of the organization are not just on the wall; they are in the hearts and minds of the team and provide direction and balance as they make decisions to move the company toward their objectives. To achieve this level of engagement requires a diligent and purposeful communication culture.

The process we utilized at EHD Technologies was to engage our leadership team to help establish what the mission and values for our company should be. We provided technical support to automotive manufacturers in multiple states and had employees working on-site at customer locations, so the challenge was to establish clarity and direction that could be communicated well to remote teams. Through the interaction and input from the leadership staff, we came up with the following mission statement: "The mission of EHD Technologies is to be recognized and respected as an organization that promotes excellence, honesty, and dedication in every aspect of life."

Excellence, honesty, and dedication were the core values we had embraced as an executive team, but we had not done a good job of clearly communicating those values to our employees in the field. Our leadership team then engaged in adding definition to the existing core values and adding some additional ones that we felt were important for our business and culture. Here are the core values we finally adopted:

- Excellence—To be extraordinary.
- Honesty—Always do the right thing and never compromise.
- Dedication—To be all-in, attitude in action.
- Integrity—Down to my innermost part, be true.
- Teamwork—Helping one another be excellent.
- Create Fun—Having a positive effect and influence on others.

At this point, we borrowed the concept from Tractor Supply and printed the mission and values on a laminated pocket card. We distributed the cards to the team and updated our website and internal documents to include the new definitions. The impact was not immediately realized, but the shift in mind-set and focus on what we defined as critical could be recognized as we continued to talk about them and refer to them in our decision-making.

Soon our sales team was handing them out to customers as a differentiator in the marketplace. Customers would inquire about the cards to show to their management. Our team members in the field could readily share what the values of the company were. The behavior of our team became more and more predictable.

Inspiring others to accomplish great things in a manner that is consistent with the company's purpose and goals requires leaders to provide clarity and definitions of those expectations, then deliver them through excellent communication. As I mentioned, Greg Sandfort deflected the credit for building the great culture at Tractor Supply, but in so doing, he demonstrated the next key characteristic to inspiring others: humility.

MEASURING OUR COMMUNICATION EFFECTIVENESS

Level 1

Manager does not provide information on why decisions are made or share frequent updates.

Level 2

Manager provides infrequent feedback on performance and decision-making strategies.

Level 3

Manager sometimes provides sufficient background to decision made and long-term purposes behind them.

Level 4

On most occasions, manager provides sufficient support to decisions and ongoing topics in the organization.

Level 5

Manager is clear and concise in developing and sharing expectations and maintaining a clear flow of information to the team. Has frequent scheduled meetings with the team and individuals.

HUMILITY

My guiding principle on humility was grafted from a study of Proverbs as a young man. King Solomon was recognized as one of the wisest and wealthiest leaders to ever rule, and some of the greatest attributes on wisdom can be found in the book of Proverbs. Proverbs 25:6–7 (NIV) states the following:

> Do not exalt yourself in the king's presence and do not claim a place among his great men; it is better for him to say to you "Come up here," than for him to humiliate you before his nobles.

The thought of sitting myself at the table with a group of leaders and being asked to move to a different table so another person could have my seat resonated with me as something I would never want to happen. I have applied this example to most every area of life and always sought to be asked to take the lead. I am certainly not the best example, but I believe this example by Solomon provides a great path to follow.

As the leader, we have to make decisions with the information given and plan the course. Another area where many leaders fail to demonstrate humility is when the results of the plan are realized. Taking too much credit when things go well and passing the blame when they do not is a recipe for disaster. Genuine leaders do just the opposite.

In Jim Collins's book *Good to Great*, he explains that the

top-performing companies in his research all had a Level 5 leader at the helm. A Level 5 leader demonstrated "a paradoxical mix of personal humility and professional will" (p. 39). He identified a situation where a Level 5 leader might be present: "Look for situations where extraordinary results exist but where no individual steps forth to claim excess credit" (p. 37).

Humility is directly connected to some of the other characteristics outlined in this book as necessary to approach legacy leadership. Putting others first requires a certain level of humility as we allow other people to prosper, sometimes at our expense. Caring for others requires humility, as it is necessary to put our feelings at risk to provide a safe and supportive environment for our team.

In the next few sections, we will discuss being genuine and mentoring, both of which require humility as well. Being genuine requires opening ourselves up to vulnerability, and mentoring requires sharing our mistakes and misjudgments with those we are trying to develop.

MEASURING OUR HUMILITY

Level 1

Manager always takes credit for success of an activity or blames others for failure.

Level 2

Manager is slow to accept the ideas of others over their own or allow others to take the lead.

Level 3

Manager tends to point to their own achievement first but does give credit to others on occasion.

Level 4

Manager usually gives credit to others contributions to the success before recognizing their own.

Level 5

Manager almost always deflects praise and appreciation to others involved in the success of the project.

GENUINE

Authentic. Real. Vulnerable.

One of the most appreciated characteristics of a leader is that of being genuine and vulnerable. Admitting that we do not have all the answers does a multitude of things:

- It provides a sense of value to those who report to us.
- It engages the team to come to the right answer.
- It removes the false impression that we know it all.
- It allows for dialogue and discussion.

According to Brené Brown, author of *Daring Greatly*, vulnerability is the point where courage and fear meet. In a society that glorifies strength and confidence, being vulnerable seems to be anti-leaderesque (I might have made this word up, but it seems appropriate).

We are expected to have all the answers, know the future, and guide our team without hesitation. The truth is that is not the expectation at all. What our team wants to know is that we are genuine.

Conducting ourselves in a genuine manner will provide the foundation required to build a trusting team.

One of the most powerful statements we can make to our team is "I don't have all of the answers, and I need your knowledge, expertise, and experience to help us make the right decision and establish the right path forward." This statement of vulnerability opens the door for much deeper emotional connection and also engages the most critical aspects of a person's being—their trust.

When our team learns they can trust us to be vulnerable and genuine with our own weaknesses, they respond in kind and allow themselves to be open with their fears and weaknesses. The circle of trust that ensues allows the team to rely on one another to establish the best plan of action for all, instead of worrying about the personal outcome and impact. There are sufficient worries to consider coming from outside of our team, and building the trust circle within our team allows us to focus our efforts on solving the external problems with full focus.

Conducting ourselves in a genuine manner will provide the spark required to build a trusting team. Without the authenticity from the leader, the team will certainly pull back within the safe walls of their self-existence and venture out only on occasion. When we provide the okay to be vulnerable, amazing things can happen. Being vulnerable opens the door for much deeper emotional connection and levels of trust that only elite teams share.

MEASURING OUR TEAM'S IMPRESSION OF BEING GENUINE

Level 1

Manager appears fake in relational concerns and is difficult to approach for support or guidance.

Level 2

Manager allows for some interaction related to team member concerns but shows lack of true commitment to take any actions on the topic.

Level 3

Manager tends to have an open door for team members to dialogue but does not seek opportunity to engage team members.

Level 4

Manager provides ample time for discussion and reflection on issues and directs focus to the team member's concern.

Level 5

Manager always seems to take time to listen and relate to the team members and reflects honest concern for the situation.

MENTOR

As we grow and develop in our career, we gain knowledge and experience through the decision-making process and watching the results of our decisions roll out in front of us. The impact of experience is nearly impossible to learn from a book or classroom environment, especially the impact on people through our decisions.

A fundamental role we should provide as a leader is that of mentor. Guiding the less-experienced team member through the assessments and angles of our decision options and predicting potential outcomes of those decisions is a valuable process we can share with multiple team members.

If we look at professional athletes, we see a steady growth of outside influence the higher they go in their careers. In high school, the athlete might have a coach or two responsible for all their knowledge and physical development. In college, the influences are multiplied with the addition of nutrition coaches, strength coaches, and position coaches. Once the professional ranks are achieved, there are even more coaches and mentors in the picture, with psychological, financial, and analytical resources added to the mix.

Oddly, in business, we see an opposite reality occur during an individual's professional growth. With each step up an organizational ladder, there are fewer influencers to support the decision-making process. It is truly lonely at the top. Unless we are deliberate in counteracting this reality, we put our future hope on individuals to make all of the best decisions with little or no outside influence.

**One of the greatest values of mentors is the ability
to see ahead what others cannot see and to help
them navigate a course to their destination.
—John C. Maxwell, author**

The role of mentor is not of a directing nature but more of a questioning nature. Pushing the mentee to assess and consider different angles of approach and potential impact requires a diverse view of the facts, situation, and desired results. Sometimes delicate prodding is needed, while in other instances direct, hard-knock questions are necessary to broaden the scope of perspective. The ultimate goal is to help the individuals we are pouring into develop their own skills and learn from the decision-making process of others to realize the best outcomes possible.

Another aspect of mentorship is related to personal and professional growth. As we spend time and energy providing professional expertise, a bond of trust and confidence will develop between the mentee and mentor. Navigating the hopes and pitfalls of a career can be challenging, and having a trusted adviser to lean on during times of crisis or opportunity decision-making can provide a wealth of strength and support to the mentee. Lifelong relationships that last well beyond the professional career are often developed through the impact of a mentor.

MEASURING OUR IMPACT IN MENTORING

Level 1

Manager does not spend time developing team members except for some business-related topics.

Level 2

Manager mentions some value to personal and professional growth but does not allocate sufficient time to make progress in this area.

Level 3

Manager provides some time and effort to benefit an individual team member's growth and development.

Level 4

Manager discusses the importance of finding mentors both internal and external to the company. Supports activities and planning for personal growth.

Level 5

Manager takes scheduled time to interact with individuals on a frequent basis, providing feedback and helping develop plans for personal and professional growth.

WHAT DOES THIS ALL MEAN?

Leadership is challenging. Effective leadership is extremely challenging. To be an effective leader over an extended period is even more difficult. To become a legacy leader, we have to begin making strides in areas where we have lasting impact on those we influence. We all have influence on others, whether we choose to or not. Choose to be deliberate about your influence rather than unintentional.

Effective leadership is about personal choices:

- ❖ I choose to be deliberate about my influence.
- ❖ I choose to give great effort every time.
- ❖ I choose to do things with excellence.
- ❖ I choose to build up others.
- ❖ I choose to take time to mentor/coach/teach.
- ❖ I choose to breathe life into others' possibilities.

Consistency is a vital element of effective leading. As we heard earlier about always being on stage, especially in today's social media proliferation, we must be diligent to be consistent. While assessing our current condition in each characteristic is a point-in-time reflection of how well we are applying the principles, our overall performance should be shifting to the boxes of higher performance.

Growth in areas where you lack experience or expertise should be the focus and discussion point with your mentor or accountability group. If you don't have a mentor or accountability group in place, I would recommend taking immediate action to establish them. If you are not growing in an area, you are dying. I liken it to walking up an escalator going down. If I am climbing the steps, I will maintain my place or even gain a little ground. If I stop climbing the steps, I immediately start going down. Personal growth is very similar.

Growth requires measuring where we are: self-assessments, feedback from our stakeholders, and developing a plan for improvement. We can't fix everything at once, so a sensible prioritization of the most important elements of the three keys to effective leadership is necessary.

Identify the principle, the characteristics of the principle that are not where you want them to be, and the actions to be taken to begin to shift your behavior toward the target. Measurable actions are key. "I am going to have a better attitude" is not a very measurable action. "I will not engage in negative conversations or negative group texts" is something that will probably help your attitude and is a measurable action.

Finally, look around you and determine if the circle of influence you are giving your time and energy to is providing the platform for you to get where you want to go. Are they the people you want to become? I am not saying you toss that group aside, but if they are not where you want to go, you have to find a group that can provide the catalyst and accountability to help you grow.

Remember this: you become who you hang out with and what you read. If you are reading this, obviously you are trying to grow. It is much harder to change your circle or add to it. Growth is painful and uncomfortable but usually well worth the time and energy. Embrace the journey in the pursuit of legacy!

THE LIFE OF CHRIST—
AN EXAMPLE OF
LEGACY LIVING

There are many great leaders throughout history that we could learn from and then develop similar traits to lead a life of legacy. From Constantine in historical Roman times, to Abraham Lincoln in America, to Mahatma Gandhi in India, to Nelson Mandela in South Africa. All these historical leaders provide living examples of how their commitment to follow their principles, while enduring hardship, struggle, and often defeat, helped realize the goals they set.

As a Christian, I am going to outline how Jesus provided the ultimate example of living a life of legacy. Jesus's whole purpose was to leave a legacy of grace and peace so that humans could have a relationship with the Father. He knew from the beginning that it wasn't about Him but about fulfilling His purpose. Jesus's instruction to us in John 13:15 says, "I have set you an example that you should do as I have done for you." In the next few pages, we will discover the traits that Jesus lived by and outline the model for us to follow and live ourselves.

When we hear the word legacy, it is often associated with personal accomplishment. The fundamental focus of this book and the point of the reflection on the life of Jesus Christ is that the pursuit of legacy is not about power, status, or wealth. Our focus is on discovering the plans that reveal the character of God and ultimately drive our efforts for the good of others. Legacy occurs when others embrace the beliefs and hopes that we have established, and they take those beliefs to levels beyond what we have achieved.

In following Jesus's footsteps, there are insightful leadership qualities He demonstrated that can dynamically influence our own leadership understanding and development. He wanted us to do as He did, and thankfully, He provided the example for us to follow.

Managing Yourself

Managing ourselves well is a precursor to being able to successfully manage others. If we don't manage ourselves well, we will certainly fall short in meeting the standards necessary to manage and inspire others. The earlier we realize the critical impact of good self-management, the sooner we will be able to excel in people-management skills.

In the life of Jesus, we see that He began personal development and time-management skills well before he started his teaching and healing ministry. There is not much recorded about His early life, but self-preparation was one thing we can see clearly in scripture.

On a return trip from Jerusalem, which was a yearly required trip for all faithful followers of Judaism, Jesus was left behind by his parents, who assumed that He had begun the journey back to Nazareth with the family caravan. Three days later, they discovered Him missing and returned and found Him sitting in the temple with the high religious thinkers of the day, simply listening and asking questions. He was only twelve years old. When He had the opportunity to speak, all who heard were astonished at His understanding and answers. The scripture closes with this remark: "And Jesus grew in wisdom and stature, and in favor with God and man" (Luke 2:52 NIV).

The vision to realize that He needed to increase in wisdom was clearly a part of his understanding. He was taking the time to prepare for what was ahead of Him. He did this at twelve and maintained this quality up to the age of thirty, when God launched Him into the public eye.

The truth about Jesus's life is the same truth for us. What we do or don't do in managing ourselves will have an enormous impact on our life's outcome. Jesus had every opportunity to develop a bad attitude toward those who mistreated Him, to waste time on insignificance, to be lazy, to neglect his Jewish culture, and to overindulge in life's pleasures. He chose to take the opportunity to grow, and through

His example of preparing himself, we can learn some exceptional insights to apply in our own lives.

Attitude (Matt. 11:29, 20:26–28; Phil. 2:5–8; Rom. 8:28)

Attitude, either good or bad, has a tremendous impact on how we approach our leadership responsibility. Fortunately, our attitude can be guided by our choices and how we approach our circumstances and expectations. We can decide to bring a positive attitude regardless of how things are going at the moment and modify our expectations from one who should be served to one who is of service to others. Our attitude should reflect whom we believe more than what we believe!

If we believe we are someone of importance, then we will expect people to treat us that way. Jesus had every right to demand respect, praise, and honor as God manifested as a man, but He chose to humble Himself (Matt. 11:29). His servant leadership model has been the mark of every beloved leader for generations. The power of wisdom and the grace of service exemplifies this model of leadership that creates a culture of inclusion and acceptance. When we engage people with an intent to serve rather than be served, our attitude is completely different. Jesus points out that man's intent is to rule over other men, but His intent was to serve, and those who want to be known as great must become a servant (Matt. 20:26–28).

A second component of attitude is directly connected to a spirit of faith—faith that God is at work and that no matter what we face, we know it is all part of a larger story being told. If things go well, we give thanks. If things seem to not be going well, we still give thanks and realize this is just a part of the path that God is leading us down and that His goodness is just as real in suffering as it is in success. This attitude allows us to find the good in the bad and to keep a forward focus on what is ahead. Scripture reminds us "And we know that in all things God works for the good of those who love Him, who have been called according to His purpose" (Rom. 8:28 NIV).

When we derive our attitude from the source of our eternal

hope rather than from our temporary circumstances, we can begin to display the character of the One we represent. If we are here to serve, we won't act as if we should be served. When we don't have to rely on our own skills to be an effective tool for the kingdom, we can relinquish the angst and fear that can impact our attitude. If we are confident that God is working all things for our good, we can express joy even when we don't feel it.

One of the most impactful insights about pursuing this attitude was taught to us by my mother, who started off every day with Psalm 118:24 (CSB Version), "This is the day the Lord has made, let us rejoice and be glad in it." She inspired us to choose daily to set an attitude of thanksgiving and focus that inspired us to believe in the best in each day. Choose to find the good and the positive in your life each day, and your attitude will reflect that choice.

Effort (Matt. 21:18; Luke 11:1, 21:37; John 10:40; Mark 3:4–5)

Good self-management means doing the things that need to be done regardless of how we feel or the difficulty of current circumstances. Giving great effort is a reflection of our internal character and commitment. While we don't control the total outcome of our work, we do control what effort we put into accomplishing what we are requested to complete. "Whatever you do, do everything for the glory of God" (1 Cor. 10:31b CSB Version).

Jesus demonstrated the importance of tending to the things that needed to be done, winning the hearts and minds of the people in the process. He was up early to meet with people or to pray. He was out at night to connect with people. He was in the temple. He was in the street. He was in the towns and villages. Even when He was frustrated (Mark 3:4–5) by the hardness and pride of the people, Jesus completed the work by healing the man with the shriveled hand on the Sabbath. By demonstrating this effort, Jesus was able to share His message of grace and hope.

One of Jesus's better-known parables is about a business owner empowering those in his service. The owner gives a portion of his resources to three individuals to manage because he will be gone for a long journey. He shares the bags of gold with each of his managers in different proportions. He gives five bags to one, two to another, and one to the last. This division is important because it probably represents the owner's past interactions with these individuals and their ability and drive. Two of the individuals take what they received and apply themselves to invest and work hard and double their assets. The third gives no effort and simply buries the money so when his boss returns, he can dig it up and give it back. Jesus's response to this last person was one of His strongest rebukes in scripture. He called him lazy and wicked. Lazy because he gave no effort, wicked because he did not do what he should have done for the person who invested in him. Lazy was personal, and wicked was for how it harmed others who would have benefited but did not (Matt. 25:14–30).

Not everyone has the same gifts and talents, but we all have the same opportunity to work hard and give maximum effort. Pray like the results are dependent upon God and work like the results are dependent upon you!

Time Management (Pray—Mark 1:35; Teach—Matt. 23; Travel—Luke 9:56; Fellowship—Matt. 9:10)

Our time allotment on this earth is finite. How we choose to apply ourselves to maximize the value and impact of that time is paramount. Effectively utilizing our time requires prioritizing, planning, and being disciplined. Time management isn't just about meetings and deadlines at work; it is also about managing work commitments to coincide with relationship priorities like God, family, friends, and community.

Jesus's life was a testament to managing time effectively and efficiently to accomplish what He was on earth to complete. Jesus knew He had a short window of time on earth to share the message the Father had sent Him to deliver. Scripture references twenty-five times where Jesus went off to pray. In this time of prayer, Jesus could make sure He was in sync with the mission of the Father and prepare for the days ahead. Clarifying priorities and scheduling time away for prayer and planning are critical aspects of effective time management. If it was a priority for Jesus, it should be one for us as well.

Relationships develop through time spent together. Throughout scripture, we read of Jesus teaching the crowds about the revelation of His truth. He also made time for fellowship with disciples and with nonbelievers in one-on-one conversations. He grew faith and commitment in those who believed in Him and brought some of those who doubted to believe by showing love through time spent together.

Jesus exemplified being at the right place, at the right time, in the right frame of mind. This is all connected to managing our time well and having a margin. A margin means we are not keeping our commitments so packed that we don't have time to take the opportunity when it comes along. Almost half of Jesus's miracles happened on his way somewhere. It was the interruptions that actually became an integral part of how He lived His life. Having a margin as a part of our story will allow similar opportunities for divine appointments not on our calendar.

Managing our time through clearly defined priorities, dedicated prayer time, careful planning, and balanced commitments will allow for the necessary margin in our schedule.

Commitment (Matt. 4:1; Mark 1:35; John 10:17)

Human nature's tendency is to find the easiest path. Success is often realized by doing things that others are not willing to do. The truest test of our commitment comes in whether we are in place to serve or to be served. Jesus told the religious leaders that He came to lay his life down of His own accord. Our commitment must take similar shape in that we lay down our lives, desires, plans, and wants to help those we serve.

Commitment is one of the greatest fundamentals we need to succeed in life. Commitment leads us forward against all adversity. Commitment drives us to do the things that others are not willing to do. Commitment is the difference between excellence and mediocrity.

Jesus expressed this one leadership quality as much or more as many of the ones we have discussed. His commitment to give His life as a sacrifice was expressed daily. He chose to leave the authority and splendor of His deity and come to earth in the form of man, submitting Himself to the highs and lows of a broken world. Jesus knew the message would not be received by all and that, in the end, He would be ridiculed, insulted, and eventually killed. But He was all in for us to have communion with the Father. That was commitment. Commitment empowered Jesus to make difficult decisions with ease because commitment led the way of choice. It was always what was best for humanity, not what was best for His self-preservation.

Jesus's invitation to us was the same one He took on Himself. Mark 8:35 says, "For whoever wants to save their life will lose it, but whoever loses their life for me, and for the gospel, will save it." Committing to a cause that requires us to live a life of sacrifice is something that not many people would subscribe to. We must choose to follow His example and commit to whatever is required to achieve our ultimate objective.

Living a life of excellence is not easy, and scripture tells us that to live a life after Christ will be a challenge. Being diligent through the difficulties, taking on the hard challenges, and serving others to fulfil our calling in Christ will help us lead a life of legacy. We have to decide to commit to do whatever it takes to complete our purpose.

Policies (Matt. 5:17, 8:9, 17:27, 22:37–40; John 10:22–23; Luke 6:6)

Rules and regulations, yada, yada, yada. Why do we even have them? Rules, regulations, and policies are the fabric of how we choose to interact with one another. Even in the Garden of Eden, God laid out some policies for Adam and Eve on how to interact with Him and nature. Established policies are a component of order and structure.

Policies and regulations provide the ground rules for our interaction with others, both in the work setting and in social settings. Jesus did not need to adhere to any of humankind's policies, but in an effort to relate to us, He did anyway. He attended the traditional feasts that the Jewish ancestry had established and that were expected by Jewish law. He paid taxes to the Roman authorities as was in place at the time. On the Sabbath, He was in the temple and the synagogue, as was the Jewish custom. Jesus even recognized the faith of the centurion who operated in a strict code of policies and procedures.

As we relate to policies today, the important thing to understand is the context of why they are given. It is setting up a standard for all to work by to bring cohesion and direction. When Jesus was asked about following the rules, he took the concept to a different level and made it not about the rules necessarily but about the people affected by the rules. The simple direction Jesus provided was to have a relationship with God, and from that foundation, grow relationships with people. All the laws work if you do those two things well (Matt. 22).

Basically, adhering to the law is simply driven by a love for God and people. Policies and standards are established to create order and a framework for how people treat one another. When we realize our commitment to the policies is an expression of love rather than a point of obedience, we can truly serve those in our organization.

Energy (Luke 19:45–47; Matt. 17:17, 26:37–45; John 14:9)

Managing our energy is one of the most important things we do in this life. We all have the same amount of time to work with, 168 hours in a week. Learning to take advantage of this time requires having the mental and physical energy to perform with excellence. Therefore, we are called to take care of our bodies and our minds, just like Jesus.

Jesus exerted significant amounts of energy both physically and mentally during His time on earth. He practiced the art of skilled energy management. To accomplish all that He had to do in just three years, Jesus was deliberate about being prepared for His mission.

Jesus exercised. What we often forget about this time was that travel was primarily by foot. Jesus and His disciples went from town to town sharing the good news. After Jesus spoke to the centurion in Capernaum, the next reference in Matthew is in the town of Nain, some thirty-two miles away—a full day's journey on foot. Needless to say, Jesus was in premium physical shape, which allowed Him the energy to focus on what was most important, sharing the hope and salvation offered by God.

Jesus ate well. The food available to Jesus was what you would get from an organic grocery story today. We have to regulate what we eat today to maintain a healthy lifestyle. He also gave thanks to God for the sustenance and energy the food provided.

Jesus set aside time for rest. It is mentioned many times in scripture that Jesus took time away from everyone to get refreshed mentally and physically. We see that Jesus also practiced prayer and meditation, as was the Jewish custom. This practice is specifically designed for energy rejuvenation.

So, we see the three components of an energized body and soul that Jesus modeled are physical and mental rest, healthy eating, and exercise. In our culture of fast food, media entertainment, and excessive food choices, we have to manage what we take in our bodies and minds. We have to choose to be bodily fit as well as to give our minds rest from constant stimulation from TV, internet, and mobile phones. When we bring balanced energy to our team, they can be motivated and inspired to respond to our energy.

Mission / Vision / Core Values (Luke 4:21; John 10:15; Matt. 22:37–40)

Mission clarity provides guidance to all involved regarding what we are doing now. Vision clarity provides guidance about where we want to go and what we want to become. Clarity about the core values defines how we will act to accomplish the mission and vision. By faithfully living out the core values, we provide a lasting example for our team to follow as we pursue the mission and vision.

In Luke 4, after Jesus endured the temptation of Satan, at the very start of His earthly ministry, He arrived back at a local

Jewish synagogue and opened up the scroll of Isaiah to a prophecy concerning the messiah. He read it aloud and said, "Today this scripture is fulfilled in your hearing," clarifying His mission while on the earth. "The Spirit of the Lord is on me, because he has anointed me to proclaim good news to the poor. He has sent me to proclaim freedom for the prisoners and recovery of sight for the blind, to set the oppressed free, to proclaim the year of the Lord's favor" (Luke 4:18–19 NIV).

The vision for Jesus was also clearly established when He shared that "whoever believes in Him shall not perish but have eternal life" (John 3:16 NIV). This vision was that none would perish but that all would come to believe in the gift the Father had sent. He reminded those who followed Him multiple times, sometimes with a short version of the mission, "To seek and to save the lost" (Luke 19:10 NIV). This mandate now led Him to do all of the things He did while on earth.

Along with the mission and vision, he also established core values. These values would define the way Jesus and the disciples executed the mission and vision. Jesus pointed out two main core values: "Love the Lord your God with all your heart and with all your soul and with all your mind. Love your neighbor as yourself" (Matt. 22:37, 39b NIV). Later, Jesus added other characteristics in His Sermon on the Mount, where He established the values of self-sacrifice, humility, and even caring for your enemy as a new way of living. Judging others was put to the side, and loving others was put on the forefront. These core values helped guide the disciples to reach that generation and provide the framework for how we should live today. It is imperative that we live out the core values in our own lives to set the example.

We deliver the strength to the mission / vision / core values when we stand by them and don't waver from them. When we have the opportunity, we can reinforce why we do what we do. Holding to the mission/vision and core values even when others don't seem to grasp their importance is paramount to our leadership influence. Our example is the pathway to creating expectations.

Manage Others

Managing others well is a stepping-stone to being able to influence and inspire those in our circle of responsibility. Treating people with respect, regardless of their position or status, is a foundational aspect of good managing. We can learn from the life of Christ through His interactions with different characters and personalities, all while delivering the message and driving home the key points He was trying to make.

Jesus utilized situations and opportunities to clarify His purpose and to steer his disciples and those following Him. Even though He had the authority and power to direct people to do certain things, as we managers can, He wanted people to decide for themselves to take action. He wanted them to buy in to the message and embrace the changes that needed to occur.

Jesus was purposeful in using everyday happenings to point out the shortcomings of humanity or to show His disciples where their true focus should be. Our objective as a manager is to teach our team the proper way, lead them with intent and purpose, get them to buy into the mission and vision, and ultimately have them adopt and promote the prescribed way of doing things. Good managing is the gateway to accomplish this objective.

Communication (Matt. 5:3–12 [Beatitudes]; Matt. 6 [How to Pray], John 21:15–17 [Feed My Sheep])

Managing other people well requires a keen focus and emphasis on communication. Particularly important aspects of communication are defining guidelines and expectations we want our team members to uphold. Once we clarify the expectations, we can then focus on behaviors that will produce the results we want. By establishing the guidelines in which we are expecting our team to operate, we create a platform of reference that is not of personal conflict but of accountability to the standard. What gets measured gets managed.

In Jesus's Sermon on the Mount, He outlined the standard for living as a servant of God. Be meek, hunger and thirst for right living, show mercy, and have a pure heart. These were all aspects of the life Jesus wanted His disciples to live. Later, He calls back to these standards when He shows the Pharisees or Jewish leaders where they have replaced truth and substance with ritual and formality.

Not only did Jesus point out the standards for living, but He also pointed out the best practices that the disciples should follow for maximum impact. He pointed out the importance of praying and also described how they should pray. Clarity in communication isn't only intended for discipline but also to provide needed guide rails for our team to maximize their efforts within their scope of responsibility.

Another demonstration of great communication happened between Peter and Jesus after His resurrection. Peter denied Jesus and was distraught and downtrodden due to his foretold failure. Jesus engaged Peter at the lakeside and outlined for him what his priority and focus should be going forward. Rather than focusing on what happened in the past, Jesus shifted Peter's focus to what was the most important thing for him to do from then on—teach the followers of Jesus (John 21). Jesus knew the coming days would require a shift in focus for Peter and the disciples. Communicating well even after failure can inspire and motivate our team to a path of recovery and purpose.

Providing direction, behavioral clarity, and defined priorities are critical components of managing others well. When we focus on clear communication, we spend less time helping our team grasp the purpose of the expectations and more time on executing the outcomes we desire.

Praise (John 1:47 [Nathanael]; Mark 14:9 [Woman with Perfume])

Recognizing character and behaviors that are in line with those traits we are promoting in our organization is a powerful ally in managing people well. Whether that is a public recognition of accomplishment or a private validation of the behavior, taking the time and making the effort to confirm someone's contribution is extremely valuable.

When Jesus was first calling His disciples to join Him, He went to Galilee and called Philip to join them. Nathanael was from the same town as Philip, so Philip told him of the news of Jesus and brought him along. As Nathanael approached them, Jesus declared to the group, "Here truly is an Israelite, in whom there is no deceit" (John 1:47 NIV). Jesus's words of affirmation purposely stirred Nathanael's heart, and Nathanael confirmed Jesus as the Son of God immediately following this confirmation of character. Nathanael became one of Christ's disciples.

Multiple times throughout Jesus's ministry, He encountered those seeking Him for healing or guidance. On a few of those occasions, He commented to them, and all who were listening, on their demonstration of great faith. This recognition of faith was always followed by Jesus granting them the answer to their request (Matt. 8:6, 15:22).

A few days before his final Passover meal, Jesus was eating in Bethany at Simon the leper's home. An unnamed woman came to the house and poured perfume on Jesus's head. Those in attendance rebuked her and spoke harshly to her actions. Remember, in this time, women were not treated with equal respect as men, but Jesus called out her action as a special gift. Recognizing people who are in the background and not just the front-runners is a trademark of great management and leadership.

Jesus utilized the power of praise to recognize those individuals who demonstrated important characteristics and behaviors that validated His message. He recognized the lowly as well as the powerful, the meek and diligent, and the humble. His praise reinforced the actions that pointed people to the character of God. Affirmation of desired behaviors or character leads to increased adoption of that behavior.

Team Building (Mark 3:7, 4:34, 8:10; John 6:3, 18:1–2)

When people spend time together both in a work setting and away from work, the opportunity to develop team cohesiveness is created. A healthy team can be defined as a group of people who trust one another and are working toward a common goal. A team provides strength and encouragement to its members by supporting and motivating each one to accomplish the goals set forward.

Jesus knew that His disciples would need to grow strong bonds with one another to handle the challenges and struggles that would be a part of following Him. Scripture references a number of times when Jesus was in the temple teaching the masses along with His disciples. Other times, Jesus took the disciples to private places to pour into them more wisdom and clarity than He would share with the public. In these moments, the disciples could grow their relationships with one another.

In Mark 3, Jesus withdrew with his disciples to the lake after being in the synagogue. In Mark 4, scripture tells us Jesus would explain the parables He used with the crowds when He was alone with His disciples. In John, Jesus takes the disciples to an olive grove in the Kidron Valley to prepare for his arrest. Scripture confirms that Jesus was deliberate about getting away with the disciples.

One of Jesus's most powerful leadership principles was taught in a team-away moment when two of his top leaders were discussing who would be second to Jesus in authority when He became ruler. They had a false assumption that Jesus was going to Jerusalem to use His supernatural power and authority to establish Himself as the new ruler of the world. When Jesus responded to their comments, His words of leadership established a new standard and mode of operation for the entire team. He flipped leadership upside down. It had always been true that whoever was in charge got to have things their way. Jesus taught them about a new standard of leadership that we call servant leadership today. The first will be last; the leader will serve his followers (Mark 10:42–45). Jesus used Himself as an example by showing that the person who was in charge must be willing to suffer first to save the rest. Jesus was able to clarify His purpose and validate the expectation for His disciples to do the same through these escape moments.

Time away from the normal work setting allows for more intimate connection and moments for the team to bond. Facilitating time away for our team as a normal practice fosters opportunity for growth in trust, commitment, and relationship strengthening that is seldom achieved in the usual environment. Validation of purpose and priority can also be accomplished through this time away with your team.

Teach and Coach (Luke 10)

Taking the opportunity to highlight the importance or relevance of a situation is often maximized through the function of teaching and coaching. A higher level of respect and access is gained through developing relationships with our team members, helping us earn the opportunity to speak into their hearts and minds. Moments of opportunity are solidified in the character of those under our instruction through these intimate interactions of thought, purpose, and emotion.

A coach teaches how it is to be done and then releases you to attempt to do it the way you were instructed. A good coach follows up with you to examine how you are doing and to make sure that you are on the right track. We see the perfect picture of this in Jesus when He released the disciples to go and heal the sick, cast out devils, and teach about the kingdom of God. He had been modeling it before them, but now it was their turn to learn to exercise their own faith when ministering to people. They had learned well and returned with joy because of all the miracles that had happened. I am sure Jesus celebrated with them, but more importantly, He took this moment to refocus their attention on what was most important in what they were doing. The miracles, Jesus emphasized, were not about how much supernatural power the disciples revealed they could operate in but about how this would impact others' spiritual journey toward a relationship with God (Luke 10:1–18). Good coaches inspect what to expect.

All through the scriptures, Jesus utilized parables and stories to connect individuals to the precept or key point of His message. In the parable of the Good Samaritan, Jesus created individuals in the story that each person listening could connect with, either hypothetically or actually. The end of each story leads to a reflection on the key behavior or belief that He wants the listeners to assess in their own lives. His directive after the expert in the law declared the Good Samaritan as the true neighbor was to "Go and do likewise" (Luke 10:37b NIV). It was a solid teaching moment of which Jesus took advantage.

Teaching and coaching opportunities are seldom scripted. Being diligent about recognizing when one presents itself will help you take full advantage of those opportunities to grow and develop your team. Check up on the things you want your team to be doing and validate them when they accomplish the desired performance. Find the proper way to connect each team member to the mission and vision so that when the time comes, the value of the instruction can have deep impact.

Accountable (Matt. 25:14–30 [Talents], 25:1–13 [Bridegroom], 26:40 [Pray for One Hour])

Holding people accountable for behaviors and performance can be challenging. This approach seems to be in contrast with the other aspects of being a Christ follower, such as love and forgiveness. As mentioned before, establishing clear standards and expectations is a key step to holding people accountable to performance. Jesus demonstrated love and forgiveness but also called out behaviors that didn't align with the truths of the Gospel or didn't live up to His expectations.

In the parable of the talents, Jesus outlined for His followers that it was not okay to do nothing with what they had been given. The expectation is set that we are to utilize the gifts we have to bring value to others, especially bringing the opportunity to know Christ personally. He went so far as to chastise the servant who did nothing with the talents by calling him lazy and wicked.

At the Garden of Gethsemane, Jesus was distraught with what was being asked of Him, and He broke away to engage the Father. He asked Peter and the brothers, James and John, to go with Him to keep watch and pray. He went on a little farther and came back some time later to find the disciples asleep. He challenged them by asking, "So, couldn't you stay awake with me one hour?" Two more times, Jesus went to pray, and the disciples fell asleep each time. Jesus called them out for not being able to stand firm to the expectations.

Additionally, Jesus points out that there are consequences for not meeting the expectations that are established. Our society is one that wants a high level of grace and acceptance but wants a low level of accountability and responsibility. In the story of the ten virgins, Jesus points out the foolish virgins did not prepare for the wedding banquet. While the groom tarried before picking up his bride to go to the wedding ceremony, as was the custom in those days, the foolish virgins ran out of oil for their lamps. While they were away getting more oil, the bridegroom arrived, and the wise virgins went into the wedding banquet. Those who were not ready, who had gone away to get more oil, were not allowed to be reunited with the wedding party. Poor planning and execution can exclude us from the expected reward.

Jesus held the disciples to a high level of accountability while He was with them. The main reason this was necessary was because He knew they would be responsible for bringing the truth of heaven to earth after His ascension. They needed to be ready for what was coming. In essence, accountability is preparing others for succession or future success. Preparing those we serve to live at the level of expectancy that has been established requires diligent accountability.

Motivate (Matt. 11:28–30 [Yoke Is Easy]; John 16:31–33 [Overcome the World]; Luke 12:12 [Holy Spirit])

There are always difficulties and challenges to face—relational challenges, physical challenges, emotional challenges, spiritual challenges, and even opportunity challenges. Motivating our team to lean in during those challenging times rather than turn away can help them overcome and achieve more than they thought possible. Often, making a change in attitude or behavior is critical to getting through the difficult seasons.

Embracing change is a very difficult task for people. We like what we like, and so do the people who work for us. Helping people see the purpose and reasoning behind accepting change takes motivation, strategy, and repetition. Jesus knew His message would be a hard one to accept for many Jews, but He provided ample justification for them to accept Him as the Messiah. He performed many miracles and highlighted where scripture from the Old Testament was fulfilled in His coming to earth.

Jesus knew the disciples would face difficult times after He was resurrected and returned to the right hand of the Father. Just prior to Jesus's arrest, He was with the disciples preparing for the Passover festival, and he told them of the time to come. He warned them of the pending struggles and how they would be scattered, but He also shared with them the wisdom and powerful message that they would need to be successful in their mission. "In this world you will have trouble. But take heart! I have overcome the world" (John 16:33b NIV).

Jesus not only addressed the fears of His disciples about the physical victory He had already won, but He also provided a hope for the spiritual support that would come with the Holy Spirit. Jesus helped the disciples accept the circumstances of His departure and change their focus from being discipled to discipling others. Jesus changed the perception of their lives from the earthly to the eternal.

Jesus directed the focus of the disciples by continually placing the goal of bringing God's kingdom to the earth as the number one agenda. He talked about a kingdom that was greater than the here and now and worth living and dying for. In his famous lesson on prayer, Jesus emphasized "Thy kingdom come, Thy will be done in earth as it is in heaven" as a daily conversation for living (Matt. 6:10 KJV). Living a life of purpose is one of the most powerful motivators. Jesus provided the purpose for the disciples to embrace and follow.

Jesus motivated His team through wisdom, plan of action, and repetition. We can follow His lead in helping our team grow their passion and desire by providing personal and spiritual growth tools and guiding them to a purposeful and successful season with us. What we say, what we plan, and what we do motivates our team to focus on the primary purpose and adopt change in their own lives.

Care (Matt. 14:14 [Compassion]; Mark 10:46–52 [Heals the Blind Man])

It has been said that people don't care how much you know until they know how much you care. Care is an emotional connection to people that builds trust, commitment, and loyalty. Additionally, when people realize your intent is to help them and not just take from them, they are more willing to listen to your direction and embrace your vision.

By His very nature, Jesus cared for people. After learning of John the Baptist's death, Jesus left by boat to a solitary place. The people heard of where He had gone and followed Him. When Jesus came to the shore, He saw the crowds there waiting for Him and had compassion on them and healed their sick. Shortly after this, Jesus directed the disciples to feed the many thousands of people who had come to see Him. Knowing they could not get enough food to feed them all, Jesus fed the five thousand with five loaves and two fish—a miracle of care and compassion.

Jesus had many people following Him and asking for His time and for teaching and healing. On many occasions, He stopped the masses to address an individual. On His way to Jericho with the disciples and many other followers, the blind man Bartimaeus was by the road they were traveling. Rather than ignore the pleas of the blind man that the locals had come to drown out, Jesus stopped and engaged him. Jesus healed the blind man, and he immediately became a follower.

Taking time out for the individual demonstrates care, builds trust, and strengthens the bond between the two parties. When we study the scriptures, we see that almost half of Jesus's miracles were done by what we would consider interruptions to His plans. We can actually see that these interruptions were the gifts that God sent to establish His care for the people and reveal who Jesus was to the world.

Jesus's care for humankind was repeated time and again through His miracles and His willingness to engage the individual where they were. Caring for others comes in many forms, but the most effective demonstration of care is through action. Jesus modeled care for this world and for individuals by taking the time to understand what people were going through and meeting their needs, often interrupting His plans. We can demonstrate this same care by being aware of opportunities, taking time from our full schedule, and then taking action to meet people's needs.

Policies (Matt. 17:24–27; John 10:22–23)

One of the most challenging and least desirable aspects of managing other people is holding our team to the established policies and procedures. Often these policies are not ones we created, and we may not totally agree with them, but they are in place, and it is a part of our duty as managers to uphold the established rules.

Arriving in Capernaum, Jesus and His disciples were approached by the tax collectors regarding the traditional temple tax. He addressed Simon, who was with Him, about the sensibility of the tax and made His point to the tax collectors as well. But, in respecting the laws of the time, Jesus had Simon pull the coins out of the mouth of a fish and paid the tax! Even though Jesus knew the tax was a ritual made by humans, He knew the spiritual value of adhering to the law.

Jesus had come to fulfil the law and certainly had the authority to bypass any of it. Consistently throughout scripture, you read of Jesus adhering to the customs of the people by attending the various ceremonies held throughout the year. In John 10, Jesus is observing the Feast of Dedication, walking in Solomon's colonnade in the temple. By participating in the ceremony, Jesus was given the opportunity to speak to the religious people about the truth of who He was and how the Father had sent Him.

The most important part of what Jesus stressed when He did follow the guidelines of the day was the extreme importance of placing God in equal esteem. In one of His conversations with the critics of the day, who were trying to trap Him concerning an imperial law on paying taxes, Jesus had an opportunity to push off a local policy. Jesus ends the conversation with great wisdom when He simply states, "Give back to Caesar what is Caesar's and to God what is God's" (Mark 12:17 NIV). In other words, do the right thing by your company while still doing the right thing by God's standards.

Jesus's focus was to honor the policies while caring for the people. In Matthew 23, Jesus addressed the Pharisees, the managers of the day, about their moral imbalance. The Pharisees focused on the visible points of service, such as tithing and public prayer, but disregarded the more important aspects of the law: justice, mercy, and faithfulness. Jesus reminded them and the crowds that what was most important about their adherence to the policies were the matters of the heart.

By holding Himself and the disciples accountable to the laws in place, Jesus earned the opportunity to speak into the hearts and lives of those who were doing the same, and some who were not. People will analyze our behaviors as it relates to policies, even things we may not agree with. But if we demonstrate a willingness to follow them anyway, we provide a platform in which to influence the lives of those under our stead.

Inspiring Others

True leadership is measured by the performance and results of those directly trained and influenced by the leader. The difference between a Level 4 leader and a Level 5 leader, according to Jim Collins's *Good to Great* definition, is the success the Level 5 leader sustains even after they leave. Level 4 leaders influence the results only while they are still there.

Preparing the team to take over and lead the organization to new heights is a main objective for leaders focused on the right things. Inspiring others to do more than they thought possible, to take on more responsibility than they thought they could handle, and to carry forward the purpose and values of the organization are traits of legacy leadership.

Jesus's time in ministry on the earth was only three years. During that time, He had to reveal His true identity, identify His disciples, and prepare them to spread the good news of His coming to the world. With such a limited time to complete all that He had come to do, Jesus was very deliberate about his interactions, even from a young age.

Jesus's interaction with His team was built around preparing them to complete the purpose for which they had been called. Their new purpose was to go and make disciples of all nations, baptizing them and teaching them. We will see through scripture how Jesus demonstrated the characteristics that prepared and motivated the disciples to meet the challenge.

Others First (Matt. 20:28 [But to Serve]; John 3:14–16 [God So Loved])

Enduring influence happens when we focus our thoughts, efforts, and energy on helping others accomplish their goals and dreams while fulfilling our common mission. When our team experiences and receives the benefit of our action without regard for credit or recognition on our part, they go out of their way to make sure their contributions to the organization are completed with excellence. When you have a team of people performing their tasks with this dedication, truly exceptional results can be realized!

Jesus's principle of others first is expressed from the first miracle recorded in scripture to His ultimate sacrifice on the cross. The first miracle was for His mother. She asked Him to help a friend at a wedding who had run out of wine. Jesus's first response to her was "Not now, Mom." But she knew her Son and how He could not help but put others ahead of Himself. He took care of her needs and the needs of all at the wedding by turning the water into the best wine ever made.

Jesus's whole existence on earth was about others. In John 3, God reveals His love for the world by sending Jesus, His Son, to offer eternal life to all. Jesus knew His life was for others, and He wanted the disciples to embrace this same purpose. His focus during the three years with the disciples was transforming their thoughts from themselves to others. They eventually realized that Jesus came to give eternal life to those who accepted Him and that He was preparing them to bring as many to faith as they could.

Another beautiful thing we find out about our human existence is that we experience complete joy and fulfillment when we give of ourselves for the benefit of others. When we do things for other people and don't gain a direct benefit from the actions, we are free to receive the emotional and spiritual renewal the giving provides us. It seems that we are more open to hear and receive from the Holy Spirit when we humble ourselves in such a way as to serve with no regard for reward.

When we put the needs and wants of those who work for us ahead of our own goals and aspirations, we build an environment of trust and loyalty required for legacy leadership. This focus on others empowers them to accomplish more than we could have and creates a platform for continued growth and execution of our mission and vision.

Inspire (Matt. 4:19 [Peter and Andrew]; John 14:12 [Greater Works]; Matt. 16:18 [On This Rock])

Our primary goal as leaders is to help others accomplish more than they ever thought possible. An interesting point of note is who Jesus selected to be His disciples. He didn't select the popular, the prominent and educated, or even the wealthy. Jesus primarily chose those who were lowly in the eyes of the society to be His disciples and to carry His message. If we were to assess this group and guess whether they would be successful in their venture, we probably would have given a thumbs-down. Fortunately, God is able to use whoever is willing to accomplish His great work.

Andrew and Peter were fishermen in the area of Tiberius on the west side of the Sea of Galilee. Andrew had listened to John the Baptist and become a believer in his message of the coming Messiah. When Jesus arrived, Andrew brought his brother Peter to meet Him, and Jesus called them. "Follow me and I will make you fishers of people" (Matthew 4:19–20 CSB). Immediately they left their nets and followed Him. Peter became the voice of the disciples and the one to boldly proclaim the truth of Jesus's message after His death on the cross. Thousands of people came to believe because of the preaching of Peter.

At the Last Supper, Jesus met with the disciples and revealed to them His plans and purpose to be crucified and go to the Father. He promised He was going to prepare a place for all of them and encouraged them that the Holy Spirit was coming to give them power to continue the journey they had begun. Jesus told them that through the power of the Holy Spirit they would continue to do the works that He had done, and even greater works were yet to be performed by them. He was inspiring them to face the challenges ahead with promises of peace, comfort, and His constant presence.

Obviously, the disciples were prepared and inspired to complete the work they had been called to perform. All but one of the disciples were killed for following the leadership and calling of Christ. Today, more than two billion people claim to be followers of Jesus throughout the world. Can we inspire our band of followers to be as successful? Jesus calls us to do as He did.

Business Acumen (Matt. 24:4–5 [Don't Be Deceived]; John 14:16–18 [The Holy Spirit])

We impact the thoughts and perspectives of our team regarding the long-term mission and vision. Focusing on the big picture in our team's daily actions and decision-making requires a transition of priority and purpose.

Jesus taught the disciples to think of things in a higher way. He introduced the concept of the kingdom of heaven and the kingdom of God as the purpose for how to operate. He caused people to think beyond the temporary to consider the eternal.

One of the key concepts that Jesus taught was the power of transformation: to change what one believes and how one acts for the greater cause at hand. He taught the disciples how to grow in life. Whether it was related to money, relationships, business ethics, or interpersonal interactions, Jesus talked about a different walk than what people were used to seeing. It was the high road of life that He taught and modeled.

Jesus knew the road ahead for the disciples was going to be difficult and would require them to continue to embrace the truth of His teaching. He knew they would be questioned and challenged after His departure. Jesus was deliberate in directing the disciples to know the difference between truth and falsehood. He knew there would be false prophets that would arise and try to lead people down a path of deceit.

Finally, Jesus confirms the promise of the coming of the Holy Spirit as a key component in their mission. He refers to the Holy Spirit as the "Spirit of truth" in John 14:17. The Spirit will give the disciples the words to say and the strength to stand firm, if they will receive and embrace the Spirit.

Jesus knew that in order for the disciples to be successful, they had to be diligent about their preparation and their work. Helping our team to grow in knowledge and to focus on the big picture takes diligence and commitment. Finally, we can model the power of prayer as a component of leadership. We won't have all of the answers and need to rely on the Holy Spirit just as much as the disciples did to stay on track.

Communication (John 4:7–26 [Woman at the Well]; Matt. 13 [The Sower], 28:19–20 [Great Commission])

Communication is a fundamental component when effectively inspiring others to carry the purpose, vision, and message of our organization. Communication is an exchange of a thought, idea, or directive. It is a message given and a message received. Jesus utilized various skills and methods to reveal Himself to the world and to highlight how people should live and serve others. In the following examples, Jesus engages both believers and nonbelievers in dialogue about themselves, about Him, and about truths in their lives. His conversations are more than mere discussions. They are deliberate interactions with each person to reach a point of understanding and deep meaning.

With the woman at the well, who was obviously not part of the in crowd as far as Jewish tradition and ritual were concerned, Jesus chose to reveal Himself to an outsider very early in his ministry. Jesus led the dialogue to disclose her untrue beliefs about who God is and who the Samaritans worshipped. He also revealed the truth about who He was and the path to eternal life. Her life was transformed through His honest and open communication.

One key form of communication that Jesus taught as a skill was the question. Jesus never asked a question that He did not already know the answer to. His desire for others to be involved in the conversation led Him to ask leading questions that required the answerer to contemplate before speaking. It also allowed Him to respond with clarifying wisdom. Jesus understood where they were by listening to their response, and He was able to finish leading them to the right way of thinking. This amazing skill is what helped people get clarity on what Jesus really meant.

Jesus utilized the power of storytelling (parables) to maximize the individual impact achieved through His teaching. In the parable of the sower, Jesus described different scenarios that people could certainly relate to in a farming/agricultural community. Each person in the story received the message in a different manner. He then tied the behavior of individuals to the situation of their hearts. He made them think about their commitment to the big picture. Do you hear what I am saying? He wanted people to understand the message.

Jesus's final directive was outlined to the disciples in Matthew to go and make disciples of all nations. This is the command where the legacy of Jesus's purpose and time on earth was realized. The beauty and love of His message were carried across all continents by His disciples. Our instructions should be similar in scope and purpose to our team: commit to the purpose and values of our organization and spread the reach of that commitment wherever you interact.

Humility (Matt. 20:26 [Servant], 26:53 [Gethsemane]; John 6:38 [Father's Will])

When we are slow to take praise and quick to dish it out to our team, we build a bond of gratitude and trust that builds on itself time and time again. Things were pretty much the same in the time of Jesus as they are today. The rich and the powerful are deemed successful by the amount of money they have or the influence they wield on society. As Jesus did with most of the philosophy at that time, He turned things upside down by stating that in order for one to be great, one must become a servant.

Before sharing the first communion with the disciples, Jesus once again modeled this quality. As they entered the upper room for their last meal, Jesus took each of them and washed their feet. The custom of the day was for the lowest servant of the house to be present to wash each person's feet as they walked in. When Jesus lowered himself to wash the disciples' feet, they at first declined to let Him do it. His response was direct. "I must do this for your sake." Each of them allowed Jesus to wash, and each of them felt the amazing humility of their friend, teacher, and ultimately Savior. His willingness to lay Himself down was completely expressed at the cross. It was this sacrifice that filled the hearts of His future leaders and allowed them to do the same in their time of opportunity for all who followed them.

In the Garden of Gethsemane, Jesus commanded one of His companions who had struck the Pharisee's servant with a sword to put it away. Jesus reminded them that, at His command, more than twelve legions of angels could be at His disposal, but that was not the action He took. He also reminded them of the promise from scripture that was to be fulfilled by His pending death. Jesus took no action even when He had every right to—and the power as well.

A great sign of humility is not wielding power and authority in your control, even when you have it and are justified in using it.

On the Sea of Galilee near Capernaum, Jesus again confirmed to the crowd who had found Him that His purpose was to do the will of the Father. While Jesus was God in the flesh, He also knew that His purpose was more important than what He wanted at that moment. "For this is the will of my Father: that everyone who sees the Son and believes in him will have eternal life" (John 6:40a CSB). Jesus's effort was not for Himself or His desires but to carry out the purpose the Father had sent Him to complete.

We must constantly keep an attitude and posture of service. Deflect praise to those around us and stand in front to receive criticism. The lasting impact of a team who knows their leader will model these traits will be far-reaching.

Genuine (John 3:16 [Love], 11:35 [Jesus Wept], 14:2 [Prepare a Place])

Lasting impact in people's lives can only happen when there exists trust and a true feeling and understanding of personal care. When people feel like you care for them, they are more willing to hear your advice, opinions, and guidance.

Jesus knew His disciples would need to know His heart and intentions toward them in order for them to abide by His teaching and carry the message to the nations. In John 3, Jesus is speaking at the house of Nicodemus and outlines His whole purpose was to bring salvation to those who believe in Him. The centerpiece of this agenda was God's love for all humankind. God sent Jesus to earth not to condemn them but to offer salvation.

While Jesus was here on earth, He also developed human relationships and connections. One of those close connections was with Lazarus, the brother of Mary and Martha from Bethany. The sisters sent a message to Jesus that Lazarus was sick and that He should come quickly. By the time Jesus arrived back in Bethany, Lazarus had been dead for four days. Mary met Him as they entered the town, along with many who had been mourning, and this encounter and connection caused Jesus to weep. This personal connection with Martha, Mary, and Lazarus revealed His genuine, heartfelt care for this family. He proceeded to raise Lazarus from the dead and perform one of the greatest miracles while on earth.

In John 14, Jesus provides a glimpse of what promises lie ahead for those who are faithful in carrying out the call of service for the kingdom. His description wasn't vague or mystical but realistic and comforting to His disciples. "My Father's house has many rooms; if that were not so, would I have told you that I am going there to prepare a place for you? And if I go and prepare a place for you, I will come back and take you to be with me" (John 14:2–3a NIV). Jesus is reassuring the disciples that He is genuine, and His words are true and valid, and that there is a future and a hope for those who follow Him.

There is a proverb by Solomon that states "Faithful *are* the wounds of a friend, but the kisses of an enemy *are* deceitful" (Prov. 27:6 KJV). Being genuine means being honest even if it is painful. Too many leaders sugarcoat what needs to be said instead of expressing what is necessary, ultimately missing out on the opportunity to lead someone to a new level of understanding. Jesus's care for the disciples was expressed in His ability to be totally honest with them, even if the initial experience was less than comfortable.

Jesus's need for genuine relationships led Him to be candid while at the same time sensitive to their needs. This skill, when mastered, builds trust and deep respect. We must demonstrate the same boldness and empathy when engaging our team.

Mentor (Mark 5:37, 9:2, 13:3)

Walk a mile with me. The saying is a metaphor for doing life with someone else—experiencing with someone the highs and lows, the questions and resolutions, and the joys and sorrows. When we walk alongside our team members, we get a chance to support them and hopefully bolster them through life's ups and downs.

In the story of Jairus the synagogue ruler, Jesus was heading to his house because Jairus's daughter was very sick. They were delayed due to the crowds, and before they could make it to Jairus's house, servants came and told them his daughter had died. Jesus told Jairus to not be afraid and just believe. He also brought Peter, James, and John along with him so they could see and experience and learn from this lesson. After dismissing all of the people who did not believe, He brought the disciples and the parents into the girl's room where Jesus brought her back to life. Peter, James, and John got the chance to see the personal impact of Jesus's miracles and were empowered to do the same when the charge came.

On another occasion, Jesus was sitting on the Mount of Olives with Peter, James, John, and Andrew when they asked Him about the coming of the end of the age. Jesus was able to share intimate details of the struggles the disciples would face in the days ahead. Being separated from the large crowds gave Jesus time to have hard conversations and explore the hearts of His disciples. Through this time of mentoring, Jesus was able to encourage and prepare them for what they had been called to accomplish.

Jesus also took Peter, James, and John up on a high mountain where they could be alone. At this location, Jesus was transfigured, and the disciples could see Elijah and Moses together with him. Again, by having the disciples alone with Him, Jesus was able to share some of the heavenly power that God granted Him while on earth. Peter, James, and John were willing to engage and be a part of something they didn't fully understand. They were totally committed to Jesus. While we may not perform such great displays as this, the fact that we can empower our committed team members with information or knowledge provides a stepping-stone for growth and development of those select team members.

Mentoring key members of our team requires deliberate planning and intentionality. Not everyone is ready to receive deeper truths or broader knowledge, but when we engage those who are ready, we build deep and strong relationships that can drive future growth and development.

SUMMARY

Understanding how we are supposed to lead in this life is a challenge and a lifelong journey. God the Father is too big to fully understand. God the Son gave us a living example of how to manage and lead during His time as a man on earth. With the help of God the Spirit, we can hold these truths, behaviors, and characteristics that reflect how Jesus lived His life.

Christ's example in scripture provides real efforts and activities that we can model in our own managing and leading. The beauty and simplicity of the review of Christ's life shows us not a theoretical view of what might work but an example of what does work and how impactful a life of legacy can be. Our task is to follow His lead!

Managing ourselves well, managing others with purpose and intent, and inspiring others through service and humility lays a firm foundation for leading a life of legacy. Knowing that our focus on great leadership is intended to lead people to a relationship with the Father, through Jesus Christ, will guide us through the difficulties and challenges of leading people well. May you be encouraged, challenged, and inspired in your own leadership journey to follow the example that Jesus gave us in pursuit of legacy.

ACKNOWLEDGMENTS

To my wife, Debbie, who for thirty years has been my motivation, my sounding board, and my partner. Without your love and inspiration, I would never have made it on this journey.

To my children, Emma, Hannah, and Daniel. Much of my toil and pursuit was to provide, motivate, and inspire you to do great things. You can become all you want to be.

To my brother Bill, who helped bring the life of Christ into real, practical living examples. His wisdom and insight made the book more than I imagined it would be. To my brother Chris, whose journey was so similar to mine; we bounced things off each other for many years.

Mom, for your never-ending prayers and love for me on my journey. Tony and Kathi for helping to shape me and motivate me. Bob 'Pop' who taught me many of the principles in this book. Chester and Ellon who supported us at every turn. Jan, Jamie and dad, who encouraged me on my pathway. To my business partners, mentors, friends and extended family who have made so many contributions to me and my journey.

Dewey Greene, your insight, experience, and encouragement have been instrumental in me getting to this point. I am forever grateful for you and all of my C12 board members who helped me be a better leader, a better husband, and a better father. Mark and John, our friendship and shared life experiences have been sources of joy and support for nearly thirty years.

Mike Huffman, our partnership and friendship has meant

so much to me, and much of what is in this book came through our learning how to run and grow a business. Aaron Kisner, your commitment and dedication from almost day 1 of EHD helped us stay the course through ups and downs. Jeff McKeehan, your business and leadership insight helped me transition from small to big thinking. Aaron Adcock, not only your contribution in the book but also your positive and passionate approach to leading provided a great example. Jeff, Tim, Marsha, Laura, and all the staff at EHD who helped build a great place to work and hopefully influenced people for good during their time with us.

Most importantly, to my Savior and Lord Jesus Christ, who made a way for us to be saved and modeled a way for us to live. May any legacy credit I receive point to You.

ABOUT THE AUTHOR

Michael Claudio is an entrepreneur at heart, having started and built several businesses. He currently is the president at Guardian Strategic Wealth Planners, a company partnering with business owners to protect and grow their resources for greater impact.

Michael is an engineer by degree and spent more than twelve years working at OEM plants for Nissan and Mercedes-Benz in design validation and quality engineering. With escalating responsibility over the years, he left his last position at Mercedes with a staff of twenty engineers and fifty quality team members to start EHD Technologies in 2002.

EHD Technologies provided contingent engineering resources to automotive companies throughout North America. In 2009, EHD expanded into the quality-control service functions and in 2012 launched a technical staffing division. The company was recognized by *Inc.* magazine as one of the top five hundred fastest-growing companies in the United States in 2013 (#381) and 2014 (#443). EHD grew to more than five hundred permanent and temporary staff until the company was acquired in 2017.

Claudio then worked for the company that purchased EHD as COO of the Quality Services Division, consolidating five business units with more than one thousand employees working on a weekly basis.

Michael currently lives in Brentwood, Tennessee, a suburb of Nashville, with Debbie, his wife of thirty years. They have three grown children.

He serves on the advisory board for Vital Families (vitalfamilies. org), an organization designed to strengthen the modern family with hope and purpose. He also is a committed supporter of Triptych Foundation, an organization leveraging charitable funds to support media projects with a positive social message.

Michael is available for engagement opportunities in speaking, coaching, training, and consulting.

InPursuitofLegacy.com

Connect with Michael!

www.linkedin.com/in/michael-claudio-4019573

Lightning Source UK Ltd.
Milton Keynes UK
UKHW010706240520
363742UK00004B/130/J